The Comfort of Little Things

Other Redleaf Press Books
coauthored by Holly Elissa Bruno

Managing Legal Risks in Early Childhood Programs, with Tom Copeland

Learning from the Bumps in the Road, with Debra Ren-Etta Sullivan, Janet Gonzalez-Mena, and Luis Antonio Hernandez

The Comfort of Little Things

An Educator's Guide to Second Chances

HOLLY ELISSA BRUNO

Redleaf Press®
www.redleafpress.org
800-423-8309

Published by Redleaf Press
10 Yorkton Court
St. Paul, MN 55117
www.redleafpress.org

First edition 2015
Cover design by Erin New
Cover illustrations © Vectoronly | Dreamstime.com
Interior design by Erin Kirk New
Typeset in Century Old Style
Printed in the United States of America
22 21 20 19 18 17 16 15   1 2 3 4 5 6 7 8

Library of Congress Cataloging-in-Publication Data
Bruno, Holly Elissa.
   The comfort of little things : an educator's guide to second chances /
by Holly Elissa Bruno. – First edition.
      pages cm
   Includes bibliographical references.
   ISBN 978-1-60554-409-0
1. Teachers–Psychology. 2. Motivation in education. I. Title.
   LB2840.B78 2015
   370.15'4–dc23
                          2014046433

Printed on acid-free paper

For Marina: despite every setback, you find courage to seek your heart's home.

And for you, Bernie, for helping me remember the choice is mine.

Contents

Preface

One year ago on New Year's Eve, which is also my birthday, I made a powerful decision: to deepen my spirituality and live a truer life.

What I could see about my life in that moment was this:

I could see that I was repeating patterns and feeling ho-hum about relationships that by all rights should be life-giving.

I could see that I wanted to reclaim the promise of my life and discover how to live more deeply, meaningfully and, above all, spiritually.

What I could not see was the path ahead.

Yes, I had a happy and fulfilling life. But something was missing. Something was amiss. Something awaited me that I could not see.

That something was a second chance. It was, in fact, a life of second chances.

And so I stepped away from the known (a well-tended home by the lake, a fifteen-year relationship, my ebullient perennial gardens, my beloved yellow lab, my easy and predictable patterns) to risk the unknown.

The life that awaited me included a journey literally around the world (Boston to London to New Delhi to Jaipur to Udaipur to Mumbai to Kathmandu to Hong Kong to this day and this place).

And now I have ridden the back of an elephant up a mountainside without fear.

I have ended untrue relationships.

I have been measured for dazzling and sparkling saris.

I have moved into a house built in 1890 with pocket doors, patterned hardwood floors, and stained glass.

I have regained the courage to hear and tell the truth.

And I have written a book about second chances.

I had no idea where my quest would take me. But I knew I had to choose freedom over security, learning over repeating, and love over all substitutes.

You have had these moments, these opportunities for second chances. You offer these moments to others every day; you bear witness to a child's wonder and in so doing, open the way for a lifetime of learning. You listen to a person's struggle and hear the dream beneath the suffering. You create classrooms everywhere: on a field trip to the fire station, in the moment a child is about to strike another child, when a burdened parent walks through your door, when things don't turn out as you had planned, when you listen to your own true voice. This is the territory of second chances.

I wrote this book, *The Comfort of Little Things: An Educator's Guide to Second Chances*, for you, for me, and for every person who touches the lives of others. We deserve that second chance. We deserve

- the comfort of being unburdened;

- the encouragement to make the difference only we can;

- to loosen the limits we put on ourselves;

- to appreciate the complex marvel that we are;

- the relief in learning from our mistakes and failure;

- the comfort that flows from acceptance;

- the freedom that comes from no longer harshly judging ourselves and others; and

- to be honored and protected and soothed.

As you let yourself find the second chance in each moment, especially in those anxious moments, you model hope for others. You model compassion. You model forgiveness. You model how to learn. And yes, you model how to laugh at yourself, get over yourself, and grow.

If we let go of the life we have planned, we regain the life we are meant to live.

Each of us each day, each moment, has a choice: give ourselves and others a second chance or turn away. We can be expert at keeping busy, looking out for others and neglecting ourselves. Yet we can likewise become gifted at not only offering but also accepting the wonder of a second chance.

We educators open the world to our students. Isn't it time that we open the world to ourselves as well?

Join me in a quest to discover the life that awaits you if you decide that yes, you are worthy of a second chance.

May this book befriend and support you along the way.

Acknowledgments

To Kyra Ostendorf and David Heath at Redleaf Press for reminding me that truth-telling is compelling.

To my virtual assistant, Janelle Brandon, in Canada, who, in minutes, resolves technological issues and unknots details that could have stressed me for hours.

To Dr. Paula Jorde Bloom for setting and living the highest standard of professionalism in the field of early childhood.

To each person who responded to my *Share Your Stories* blog; your stories have painted vibrant colors onto the pages that follow.

To my Twelve-Step fellow travelers for having the courage to change the things we can and for the wisdom of letting go.

To Dr. Michael Gonta, who read each of his students and teachers as insightfully and lovingly as he read his favorite books.

To Errol Smith of BAM radio network, who takes on the impossible, trusting that all good things will prevail.

To Dr. Kay Albrecht for being my fellow traveler in Chiang Mai, Bangkok, and Angkor Wat, and for memorable mornings with schoolchildren in Thailand and Myanmar.

To Ann Terrell, who persists in saying yes to advancing the rights of children, especially when she is told no and no again.

To Rich J., who views his stroke as a gift of clarity about what matters.

To my fellow educators, emotionally intelligent geniuses, who daily kick the label of "glorified babysitter" to the curb.

To you, my reader, for making a difference in children's lives, one second chance at a time.

To Simon, Shelby, and all service dogs who comfort wounded spirits.

Thank you.

Part I

An Invitation to the World of Second Chances

Chapter 1

A Year of Second Chances

When a Second Chance Calls, Will You Answer?

If you are waiting for anything in order to live and love without holding back, then you suffer.—*David Deida*

Unburdening

Life's too short to do anything but enjoy it daily.

As hardworking educators dedicated to making a difference, we, however, are easily weighed down with work and worry. Burdened with the weight of too many responsibilities, we sometimes have trouble looking up. Being burdened, we can forget what it originally meant to educate: *To draw out that which lies within* (Latin, *educare*). What lies within is our birthright to joy.

This book is about unburdening. It's about looking up. It's about choosing to take (and offer) as many second chances as our hearts can bear. It's about reclaiming the joy and humor and passion that are rightfully ours, especially when our joy, humor, and passion are under threat. It's about drawing out the promise that lies within you, me, and each person we touch.

As we do this, we find and share in all the little comforts awaiting us in our everyday lives.

What Is a Second Chance?

Through courage we do not reduce our fear, we go beyond it.

—Chögyam Trungpa

A second chance is the opportunity to come alive in the moment with the wonder of a child, witnessing people and situations as if for the first time. A second chance is an unexpected gift that takes our breath away. A second chance is a direct pathway to a grateful heart and an astonished mind. A second chance is a sacred glimpse at what is timeless and matters most.

When I ease up on my need to control outcomes and judge myself and others, I free myself to marvel. What I then see is marvelous, regardless of (or perhaps because of) how challenging it can be.

Second chances appear like a gift left at our doorstep. When we answer the door, we notice the gift and may never know who left it. Other second chances come from letting go of what holds us back. These second chances take work. But fear not, the work is always rewarded. Choosing to be open to as many second chances as your heart can bear changes everything.

Your Brain on Second Chances

Research on the adult brain illuminates the pages of this book. Without saying so directly, neuroscientists are helping us see what second chances are all about. New studies, released daily, debunk or clarify old understandings. Just when we thought we knew something for sure, we read that neuroscientists are spilling out new information to challenge the old. I find this more liberating than threatening.

The landscape of the brain is not flat. It's as complex and full of mysteries as each one of us.

Turns out our brains are wired to both avoid and embrace second chances. Turns out our twenty-first-century brains are enticed away from second chances by the allure of streaming, unprioritized information. Turns out we can make choices to find second chances both within and outside of that endless stream.

Stepping into the Unknown: Not Your Average New Year's Resolution

Perhaps because my birthday is on New Year's Eve, I'm inclined to take New Year's resolutions to heart. I don't have a choice about getting older, but I can aim to be older *and* wiser. I have known for a while that I can allow habits to elbow out creativity. Old patterns of behavior are like old friends. By relying on what I know, I can be comfortable in my ways. I know what to expect. I don't have to devote all that energy to starting over.

Okay, so life might not be as passionate or as fresh as it was when I was a wet-behind-the-ears teacher learning everything on the job or one of the small percentage of attorneys who were women in 1973. But a steady life is a predictable life. Forsythia and lilacs bloom each spring; my dog greets me with adoration at the door. My work is rewarding. My son, Nick, and I talk every evening. My friends are steady and loving. Why would I think there is more? Isn't this enough?

Sure, life as we know it is enough. But life as we don't know it? That's where the magic awaits. That's where second chances abound.

As I contemplated my New Year's resolution for 2014, I recalled in a deeper way that life is gloriously enlightening when I summon the courage to walk where I have not walked. Perhaps the time had come for this teacher to surrender to being taught in ways that I could not foresee. The time had also come for this attorney to trust the fluidly evolving spirit of the law more than the predictable letter of the law. And that is why I decided to dedicate a year to my quest to understand second chances. Along the way, I hoped to answer the following questions:

- What is a second chance?
- Where do second chances originate?
- Do we earn second chances? Do they fall into our laps, or both?
- Can we create second chances for ourselves? For others?
- Is giving someone a second chance ever "wrong"?
- What are the spiritual principles behind second chances?
- Why are second chances essential for educators and the children whose lives we touch?

I knew I would have a truckload of work in front of me, but I decided to be okay with that. Let the wild quest rumpus begin!

Where the Magic Awaits: The Worst Becomes the Absolute Best

Give Yourself a Break

If you were to make one change that would improve your life, what would that one change be?

Surrendering to the unknown can be hard, if not impossible, for me. Oh sure, I'm a free spirit. I break into song. I get a groove on when Motown pops into my head in the middle of a keynote to five hundred people. I travel the world. I meet new people to love every day.

It's a good life. And it's a complex life. We all have pain. We all have sorrow. You have your challenges. I have mine: post-traumatic stress disorder (PTSD). My nervous system craves safety and stability. My early years were a Molotov cocktail of beatings, neglect, household mental illness, and blame: "You ought to be ashamed of yourself" is one phrase I heard often that still echoes in my head sometimes.

I am not the only one with this history. Abuse and neglect are endured by more children than anyone wants to imagine. According to the Adverse Childhood Experiences Study (Centers for Disease Control and Prevention 2010), 29.1 percent of adults grew up with a substance-abusing household member; 25.9 percent were verbally abused (1611). Even one abused child is one too many.

I have taken this early unhappiness and reconstructed my life into a blessing, thanks in large part to the kindness of so many loving fellow travelers. What doesn't kill us makes us stronger, a principal from Christchurch, New Zealand, reminded me as he described the deafening earthquake that flattened his school and annihilated all records and resources. With the help of his teachers, that man picked up the pieces and created a new school that is even more effective.

I trust my life is far richer and my spirit is more resilient than they ever would have been if I had enjoyed an easy beginning. Little things delight me. I have a deep capacity for joy that balances my early experiences with sadness. Today I am grateful for all of it.

I believe I am meant to be an explorer every day of my life. Children surrounding me learn rapaciously. I learn with a similar hunger. In fact, each time I let go of thinking I have the answer, I end up loving my job as an explorer. My brain creates new pathways, and my heart opens just that much more.

So, I made my resolution to be open to a year of second chances, even if it meant I had to let go of my life preservers. Sink or swim? Okay, I would swim, even in cold, choppy waters. Robert Frost reminds me in his poem "A Servant to Servants" that "the best way out is always through." Don't get me wrong, I love my life. But I know there's more to it. I committed this year to honoring my resolution.

So began my treasure hunt for second chances. Along the way, I encountered additional questions, like these below. If any or all of these questions touch something in you, I invite you to join me in the quest for a second chance.

What would it take to:

- change your expectation of the way people should be, and find a way to enjoy them for who they are?
- forgive a person who has hurt you?
- forgive yourself when you make a mistake or fail at something that matters to you?
- flip your emotional switch to "off" when someone is pushing your buttons?
- accept that you might not be letting yourself live the life you are meant to live?
- let go of believing your solution to a problem is the only workable solution (and of course, the wisest solution)?
- be the first to wave a white flag and set aside your ego to end a standoff?
- release a resentment you have held for so long it feels as if it is a part of you?
- look around and within you to discover something lovely waiting to be noticed?
- work through your grief when you are denied a second chance in order to create your own second chance?
- wake up looking forward to each day?
- in a heartbeat, call upon humor to bring a healing perspective and lighten everyone's load?

Some people think second chances are rare and therefore precious. When a child becomes ill and then recovers, we feel like we are given a second chance to love and appreciate the child even more deeply. This is also valid: there is no moment on earth that does not hold a second chance. All we need to do is look up, notice where we are, and be open to the possibility of wonder.

Why Bother?

Our beloved world isn't always a pretty place, and some people are mean-spirited. Grave injustice still pains us. Why bother to put yourself through all the work of seeing the world anew?

Gandhi knew that "we must be the change we wish to see in the world." If I want the world to become more humane, especially to children, I need to begin by changing myself.

What choices can I make in the moment to be open to making changes for the better, regardless of my internal resistance?

Facing Up to the "Little Stuff" Can Reveal the Bigger Issues

For 2014 I decided to make a life-changing resolution that I would keep. I became willing to unclutter myself of the confining behaviors to discover more of what really matters.

What I wanted more than anything was to deepen my spiritual path. By spiritual, I mean our human desire to live a deeper, more meaningful life. For me, being spiritual isn't the same as being religious; I respect each person's choice to follow a religion's path or not.

Educators are spiritual beings—we are on earth to make a difference. We read between the lines, read people as well as we read books, and make choices that might not make sense to other people. Don't we take the "vow of poverty," for example? Instead of material riches, we choose work that will make the world better, one child at a time. As a director from Roxbury, Massachusetts, once told me: "I make decisions each day so I can fall asleep without regret each night."

I wanted to develop a closer, deeper, and more real relationship with a higher power of my understanding. In short, I wanted to stand firmly on holy ground without running away. I knew there was something spiritual about second chances, and I made a promise to myself to find out exactly what it was.

How could I do that? I established a daily practice. Again, I made a checklist:

- Begin each day by reading and reflecting on a quote or inspirational message.
- Dedicate time each week for heart-to-heart conversations with true friends and fellow seekers.
- Participate in at least one Twelve-Step meeting each week, wherever on earth I might be.
- Explore a new part of the world (India and Nepal).
- Listen to music that soothes my soul (Brahms to Smokey Robinson).
- Pray and meditate.
- Ask for help when I need it.
- Be present and open to the deeper possibilities inherent in each moment.
- Oh yes, write a book and blog about second chances.

So at sixty-eight years old, with this list in mind, I smiled, crossed my fingers, and stepped into the New Year, ready to unclutter my life in order to see what treasures and life lessons awaited me. Remarkably, one of my best friends, Marina, who had been a child care professional for more than thirty years, made a similar resolution. We decided to begin our New Year by participating in a spiritual retreat on the topic of letting go. Letting go of expectations and opening to unseen and unfamiliar possibilities, Marina and I were reminded, is a prerequisite to uncovering second chances.

Have you ever made a decision that sounded good at the time but then led to unanticipated results? One example would be the decision to give birth to, adopt, or foster a child. We can never fully predict how profoundly our lives will change when we welcome a child into our family. In fact, what I needed as a parent of young children was exactly what I would need this year: an open heart, a sense of humor, an adventuresome spirit, and courage. I had no idea how much I would need courage. I now see that changing without courage is an ornery thing. Letting go requires

*Comfort in
Little Things*

Recall your favorite teacher or someone who "got" you when you were young. Find out how to contact that person. Write, call, or show up to say thank you. Savor the moment.

trust. I was going to learn a lot about trust too. Learning to trust what we cannot see is another prerequisite to discovering a second chance.

Once in a Lifetime: A Year of Second Chances

So, this has become my Year of Second Chances. Each day I was presented with a chance to change my behavior, say good-bye to old habits, and make choices to walk into the unknown. My year has not been easy, but I would not change a thing. Each day and sometimes many times a day, we are given a second chance to live in the world anew and to appreciate life on life's terms. To take that second chance, we need to notice where we are and be open to the possibility of growing.

Come On, Join Me. You Can Do This!

So what have you got to lose? Wouldn't just one second chance sparkle up your days? Imagine a whole year of second chances. Imagine being happier. Imagine inspiring everyone around you. Imagine accepting more beauty. Imagine not only making a difference to others but making a difference to yourself as well.

    Come on. Life's too short to do anything but enjoy it daily. Find comfort in little things and joy in unexpected moments. In the words of Robert Frost's poem "The Pasture",

    I'm going out to clean the pasture spring;

    I'll only stop to rake the leaves away

    (And wait to watch the water clear, I may):

    I sha'n't be gone long. —You come too.

*This Book Is "Alive" with Readers' Stories of
Second Chances*

This book is a living invitation to you to experience
your old world as the new world it is. I say "living"
because this book is a constantly evolving partnership
with you, my readers. At any time I invite you to visit
www.redleafpress.org. Click on Redleaf Press Blog in
the middle of the right-hand column to find blog entries
for this book. Share your story. Give me permission to
include your comments, and you may find your words
on the pages of the sequel to this book! Just sayin'. . .

At the very least, the blog allows us to have a continuous back-and-forth conversation in real time. I look
forward to reading your comments!

Join me! As I glance back over my shoulder at this year, I hear the gur-
gle of so many springs, once clogged, now gushing freely. I see paths once
tangled, now cleared. I see dreams deferred, now unfolding into the path
ahead. You come too.

Chapter 2

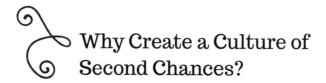 Why Create a Culture of
Second Chances?

The toughest thing is to love somebody
who has done something mean to you,
especially when that somebody is yourself.
Look inside yourself and find that loving part of you.
Take good care of that part
because it helps you love your neighbor.
—*Fred Rogers*

When Winston Couldn't Fly

Even with doctors' reassurance that preschooler Winston will fully recover
from his accident on the playground, teacher Lyra cannot forgive herself.
Lyra frets, "I knew Winston wanted to fly like a superhero; I shouldn't have
taken my eyes off him for a second! I could have prevented his leap from
the top of the slide."

Colleagues and even Winston's mom remind Lyra that her lapse of
attention in the moment Winston got hurt was an exception to Lyra's caring
and attentive nature. Everyone understands that Lyra's mom with Alzhei-
mer's had fallen over the weekend and that Lyra was checking her text
messages for caregivers' updates.

As a result of the incident, the program instituted a policy on personal use of cell phones to prevent future distractions. The program's director, Rosa, assured Lyra that if any incoming important personal calls about Lyra's mom were received, Rosa would cover Lyra's classroom so Lyra could return the call.

Regardless of everyone's understanding and support, Lyra laments, "I can never forgive myself. A child suffered on my watch because I failed to be attentive. I should have known better. Now Winston is traumatized, and it's my fault."

Lyra's Penance

Let's look at the effect of Lyra's guilt on herself and others. Assuming she failed in her responsibilities, Lyra forsakes her upbeat, optimistic, and easy-going style that children love. Her fear that another child will get hurt has turned Lyra into a hovering helicopter teacher.

Picking up on Lyra's fear, children hold back from taking risks. Their curiosity and playfulness are inhibited. Jakob worries he caused Winston's fall because Jakob was trying to get Ms. Lyra to pay attention to him, not Winston. Lyra's colleagues grow weary of her mournful, dour countenance. Winston's mother asks Rosa if Winston would do better with a different teacher.

Lyra believes she is doing the right thing by taking full responsibility for her actions. She feels she must somehow pay for her misconduct by berating herself for her failure and by becoming a more vigilant teacher. She maintains, "I cannot change what happened, but I can do everything possible to make sure it will never happen again."

Has this ever happened to you? How did you dust yourself off and move on?

> See my article in *Exchange* detailing the new policy on teachers' use of cell phones by following this link: http://www.hollyelissabruno.com/wp-content/uploads/2014/10/Hold-the-Phone-Article.pdf

How We Respond to Our Mistakes Has a Profound Effect on the People in Our Lives

Words from adults ring out like proclamations to children. We educators have powerful opportunities to model using gentle words to soothe ourselves when we miss the mark. We can model how to comfort and encourage others who might not be so gentle with themselves. Each time we model self-forgiveness, we give ourselves a second chance.

We show others how they, too, might give themselves a second chance. There is nothing admirable about damning ourselves. Working to change our behavior for the better as a result of our mistake—now that's admirable.

Sometimes I wonder if yelling at ourselves is an unwritten rule. Perhaps we have come to believe that's the only way we can learn. If that's our belief, what are our actions teaching the children?

Have Compassion. Model Compassion.

To survive the daily bumps and bruises that come with living our lives, we all need a gentle and loving home both within and outside of ourselves.

Self-acceptance in the midst of the quest to learn is a life lesson we can offer young children. In the boot camp of life, children will always need to come home lovingly to themselves, especially after failing to achieve a goal. They will always need to pick themselves up and give themselves a second chance.

Michael Jordan, whose livelihood as a basketball star required him to drive himself hard, captured the paradox of accepting failure and driving to excel in a 1997 Nike commercial: "I've missed more than nine thousand shots in my career. I've lost almost three hundred games. Twenty-six times I've been trusted to take the game's winning shot and missed. I've failed over and over and over again in my life, and that is why I succeed." High schools and middle schools around the country post Jordan's words to remind children that adults, too, can learn from our failures. In fact, some of the most successful adults are those who admit their failures and forgive themselves.

By modeling for children how to be just as loving with ourselves when we fail as we are when we succeed, we offer children a lifetime of resilience. We offer them a model for second chances.

Soulful Intelligence

When you recall your worst teacher (do this only if you are willing; memories can spark unbidden feelings), what do you recall of that person's behavior?

Can you remember that teacher's name? How you felt in that person's presence? What you learned, if anything (besides fear or anger or disappointment or how to undervalue yourself)?

We learn to define ourselves through the eyes of our teachers.

Raymond's second-grade teacher warned him, "You can't sing; mouth the words. No one wants to hear a foghorn." Raymond's singing ended on that day. Charlene's teacher told her, "Zip your lip, and for heaven's sake, stop fidgeting!" Charlene learned to be ashamed of her bubbly toe-tapping self.

Ask anyone to tell you about her worst teacher's behavior. You will witness the hurt or anger or both that still burn, no matter how many years have gone by.

If you want to witness a completely different response, ask someone (or yourself): Who was your favorite teacher? Can you tell me about her or him? How did you feel in the teacher's presence? What did you learn about yourself and about learning when you were respected for who you are? When your unique intelligences were honored?

I recall standing in the hallway beside Nelle Smither's tweed-jacketed, curly hair-haloed, wrinkled professor self as she matter-of-factly stated, "You can write." Decades later, as I dedicated my first book to Dr. Nelle Smither, I saw us again standing in the hallway on that day when she told me I could write.

No matter how old we students (of life) are, our spirit can be uplifted or crushed by a loving or dismissive adult:

- Sidney Poitier was told, "Stop wasting people's time and go out and become a dishwasher."
- Michael Jordan was cut from his high school basketball team.
- Beethoven's teacher told him he was "hopeless" and would never succeed as a violinist or composer.
- Fred Astaire was labeled: "Can't sing. Can't act. Slightly bald. Can dance a little."
- Oprah Winfrey was fired from a job because she was "unfit for TV."
- Albert Einstein's teachers said he was "mentally handicapped."

- Thomas Edison was told he was "too stupid to learn anything."
- Walt Disney was fired from a newspaper for "lacking imagination" and having "no good ideas."

Can you imagine? I'm sure you can.

"Everyone is a genius; but if you judge a fish by its ability to climb a tree, it will live its whole life believing that it is stupid," Albert Einstein observed as an adult.

IQ, EQ, multiple intelligences, standardized tests: we have created so many ways to define our intelligence, primarily from the outside looking in. Get a high enough IQ score, and you can call yourself a genius. But what becomes of the child whose genius cannot be measured?

Each of us has to find our own brand of genius, that one-of-a-kind, no-one-can-do-it-the-way-you-do-it, glowing capacity to leave the world a better place.

Fellow travelers can support you and challenge you along the way. You, however, are the ultimate expert on you. You have soulful intelligence: that inner voice that reminds you why you're here on earth and how you alone can leave the world a better place.

My friend Karen tells me she is meant to care for other people's dogs yet she questions the importance of that: "Shouldn't I do something more valuable for the world?" she worries.

Give it up, Karen. To that dog and that owner, you are the most important person. Christopher Reeve could have just been remembered as Superman. Instead, his legacy helps researchers heal spinal cord injuries.

Soulful intelligence: We all have it.

The gift is in helping each child find her voice.

The secret is in listening to our own inner voice.

The magic is in believing that what we are meant to do matters.

—Holly Elissa, September 9, 2014, from her blog

Comfort in Little Things

Take this moment to assess where stress is in your body. Are your shoulders tight? Is your jaw set? Are your eyebrows squeezed together? Breathe soothing comfort into that stressed place, and breathe out the stress.

Using our soulful intelligence helps us notice when a second chance awaits us. In each missed shot, Michael Jordan could foresee a winning shot. In each botched step, Fred Astaire must have envisioned himself gliding gracefully across the floor with Ginger Rogers. In each failed attempt at inventing the lightbulb, Thomas Edison found the inner light to begin again. In each case, the "failed" person could foresee that no restriction in the physical world can stop our imaginations from soaring.

In Little Ways

Establishing a culture of second chances doesn't need to happen overnight. We don't need to begin in a splashy or all-or-nothing way. One act of kindness or forgiveness at a time will do. Start small. When you sneeze, for example, does a person nearby—someone you might not even know—bestow a "bless you!" on your nose-wiping self?

When someone blesses my sneezing self, I smile a thank-you in her direction. I am grateful to any person who can lift an unnoticed or embarrassing moment into a smiling interaction. I get the sense that the person who has blessed me has blessed herself as well. But when we trip up, physically or metaphorically, do we say, "Bless me"?

One of my most gentle and dearest friends, who unconditionally adores his grandchildren, curses himself nonverbally in their presence when he spills or breaks something. The lesson his grandchildren pick up nonverbally about self-acceptance in those tiny moments is the opposite of what he intends.

In little ways we barely notice, we bestow blessings (or their opposite) in any moment. Our spirit, touched by that gesture, glows or recoils in response. Instead of a blessing, I so often hear, "How stupid of me!" or "Oh man, how clumsy can I get?"

These days, when I hear or observe myself ready to beat myself up (for being human and making a mistake), I aim to step back. Instead of berating myself, I can say, "It's okay. Welcome to the human race!" From that more loving and accepting perspective, I am better able to learn from the mistake. I am more ready to envision another way to approach the same challenge. In any moment, in little ways, I can offer myself another chance.

Do you play back criticisms of yourself in your head at times? I am very good at this! My mother, meaning well, used to scold me: "Sit up straight! Don't slouch!" She insisted on good posture. Her words ring in my head as I sit typing, slouching over these words. I used to "sit up straight" (a good thing) while berating myself for failing to do so (a not-so-good thing).

Give Yourself a Break

If you are still beating yourself up over a mistake you made, say or do one self-forgiving thing to ease up on judging yourself.

But what if we were to shrug it off? What would it take to let go of these little missteps and move on with our lives, feeling lighter and more carefree? This is what it means to give yourself a second chance. Remember that second chances wait like ripe peaches on a nearby tree, offering their sweetness to us for free. I snap off a peach every time I roll back my shoulders, breathe deeply, and say, "Good for me." The taste is sweet.

What We Say to Children Who Fail: Learning from Our Profession

Consider a time when you helped a child through a difficult situation, especially if the child felt bad about herself. In fact, what would you say and do with preschooler Valerie in this case study?

CASE STUDY   *Valerie*

Valerie does not like her classmate Maxwell. Valerie says Maxwell is a baby, always pouting and crying when he doesn't get his own way. She resents all the attention Maxwell gets. After all, Valerie is a "good girl," always helping her teachers. One afternoon, Valerie decides to put a stop to Maxwell's getting all the teachers' attention. Valerie whispers to Maxwell she will pinch him hard if he doesn't stop hogging Ms. Maggie's attention. Maxwell's eyes grow big as he hollers to the teachers that Valerie is being mean to him. Valerie pinches Maxwell, she is so angry he didn't listen to her. Valerie also starts to cry because she knows she shouldn't have pinched her classmate. She knows her mother will spank her when she hears about this.

What developmentally appropriate and loving approach would you take with Valerie?

Human interactions, even when they appear complex, are usually simple: each of us needs to be loved and seen for who we are. When we are not seen, not loved, or otherwise neglected, we act out. Valerie needs to be seen, appreciated, and engaged. Pinching Maxwell was inappropriate. However, the issue is deeper: Valerie needs attention just as Maxwell does, perhaps for different reasons.

The words and actions you use with Valerie that afternoon and the next day will either mend or shut down her heart. In each moment with each child, we have a second chance to let the child know we all learn, we all grow, we all make mistakes, and we all have choices. As we offer a child a second chance, we also give our heart some ease. That ease may well result in our lightening up on ourselves too. How, for example, do you think Maggie will feel after she guides Valerie through this edgy moment?

Teacher Maggie holds and comforts Valerie as her tears turn into hiccups. Brushing Valerie's hair off her forehead, Maggie says quietly, "Tell me what happened, Valerie. I'd like to hear." Valerie's tears well up again as she says, "Nobody pays any attention to me. Everybody's always helping Maxwell. But I did a bad thing."

Maggie invites Valerie to say how she feels when she doesn't get attention. Maggie affirms to Valerie that she has a right to her feelings. Maggie explains that getting your feelings hurt is something that happens to all of us. Having hurt feelings is a very natural thing, especially when you feel left out.

They then talk about other ways, besides pinching Maxwell, for Valerie to say her feelings are hurt and she needs attention too. Maggie is careful not to judge Valerie as a bad child. When Valerie is more peaceful, Maggie asks Valerie if she wants to do or say anything to Maxwell. When Valerie says, "No!" Maggie responds: "Let's do something for another child who might feel left out like you did." Valerie leads Maggie over to Lionel, one of the shiest children in the class.

The healing has begun. Valerie is not shamed. She is able to reflect on her behavior and find alternative ways to act on her frustrations. Maggie's gentle words and soothing approach have made all the difference. Valerie will have a heart memory that we hope will help her through many frustrations to come. She has learned that hurting herself or another human being is not an acceptable way to resolve conflict.

In time Valerie will come to apologize to Maxwell too. Maggie is careful not to force that apology until Valerie is emotionally ready. Children easily see through false apologies, especially a begrudging and sullen "I'm sorry!" Each child senses immediately that nothing has changed between them. No softening of the heart has occurred. No second chance has emerged. No worries, however. We always have a second chance at a second chance!

The Emergent Curriculum of Second Chances

Our curriculum in the classroom isn't just a lesson plan. To children, our behaviors, reactions, choice making, and attitudes are all curriculum. Children observe us with listening eyes and hearts, wondering, "Why is Ms. Lyra so sad? Did I do something wrong?" and imagining, "I want to be just like Ms. Maggie when I grow up. She's always so nice to me, even when I am upset."

Offering others and ourselves a second chance in the moment is the essence of "emergent curriculum." When an opportunity to forgive myself and others seems to magically surface, do I take that opportunity to go with the flow of the moment and learn from it? Or do I "lick my wounds," hold a grudge, or cop a superior, holier-than-thou attitude?

There is a soul force in the universe, which, if we permit it, will flow through us and produce miraculous results.
—Mahatma Gandhi

Whatever I model is what children learn. Stepping back in the moment takes energy and gumption. Relying on habits is so easy. Old dogs learning new tricks? Guess what, even an old arthritic dog welcomes loving opportunities and will do everything he can to please us.

What if we were to do that for ourselves, for the sake of the children for sure, but also for our own sake? Imagine how everyone around you—colleagues, families, and friends—would feel being in your presence. That's a deep benefit of giving ourselves a second chance. The whole world around us brightens.

Reflection Questions

1. Recall a moment when you soothed and comforted a child who was upset with herself. What do you remember of that experience? How did the child respond? Would you have done anything differently given some of the suggestions in this chapter? Most importantly: Are you able to treat yourself as kindly as you do a child or another adult? What holds you back from being kinder to yourself? Identify one small step you can take today to do something loving for yourself.

2. Second chances, like emergent curriculum, show up in almost every moment. Right now, for example, I am forgiving myself for getting so involved in my writing that I will not have time to work out. What the

hey! I'll claim another time today. It's okay. Are you in the midst of giving yourself a hard time about anything you have done or failed to do? If so, step back. What can you say to yourself that would be more accepting of your humanity? What could you do to give yourself a second chance?

3. We all have experienced good times and bad times in the workplace. When you think of the good times, what did those happy times have to do with acceptance, forgiveness, and second chances? When you look back at the bad times, were second chances allowed, given, or taken? What might have transformed that not-so-great time into a gentler time?

4. Take another look at the quotes by Fred Rogers on pages 12 and 14 and the one by Gandhi on page 20. Which quote speaks most directly to you? What does the quote inspire you to think about? How did both men embody second chances in their work and their lives?

5. Put yourself in Lyra's shoes. If a child were hurt on your watch, could you forgive yourself? What would it take for you to move on and learn from the experience in a healing and liberating way?

Chapter 3

Finding Comfort in Little Things: The Promise of This Moment

The past has flown away. The coming month and year do not exist.
Ours only is the present's tiny point.—*Mahmud Shabistari*

"Notice where you are," Madeline advised. "Look up, look around. Notice where you are."

Come on, Madeline! I'm sitting on a couch across from you. That's where I am. When I leave here, I'll put my head down to brave a blustery Boston January afternoon. I have work to do, calls to make, dinner to cook. The most I'll notice is a break in the traffic stream as I huddle, bundled up against the cold, waiting to cross the snowy street.

But then I thought, this is my Madeline, my mentor, who has yet to steer me wrong. So I listened.

"Look around until something catches your eye. Pay attention to that. Keep your gaze on it. Whatever it is that captures your attention, stay with it. Something is there for you. Let it find you. Notice where you are."

Yeah, Okay, Madeline. What the hey? Love you. Bye. Thanks.

In January in Boston, the sun flees the frigid sky as early as it can. I wanted to run from Madeline's warm office to my soon-to-be-warmed-up car while the sun was still trying to light the streets. The second I stepped outside, the wind swirled fresh snow around me. I took my first step toward another warm place.

Wind whistled. Snow slowed its fury thanks to the stand of sheltering, tall pine trees on my right. Grateful to them, I looked up. Something must be tricking my eye! Were those candles glowing with light on the end of each branch? Candles in the snow? Candles warm against the cold. Merry candles, bowing gracefully in the wind. I watched them, enchanted by them, my heart quiet in their glow.

Who knows how long I stood there in the wind and snow? A second? A minute? An hour? A passing shadow of a cloud dulled the candles into what they were, iced pinecones reflecting the last rays of the sun.

Thank you, Madeline, I smiled. An ordinary and almost lost moment became a found moment transcendent in light because I took the time to "notice" where I was.

My Madeline is now eighty-nine, in Chicago, and still mentoring "until they cart me away." I carry her gift in my heart. I can stop now to notice where I am in any moment, as I have in so many sacred moments. "Beauty is truth, truth, beauty, —That is all / ye know on earth, and all ye need to know," Keats marveled in his poem "Ode on a Grecian Urn." Each moment offers a second chance to be transfixed by beauty and transformed by truth.

Will you try it? When you are ready, step away from your work or your worry or your to-do list. Look around you. Pay attention to what captures your attention. What speaks to you? Notice where you are. Stay there. Witness what you can. That moment has been waiting for you to notice. "Your vision will become clear only when you can look into your own heart," psychologist Carl Jung reminds us.

Being Present Is a Present to Ourselves and to Those around Us

I learned something again today as I watched a burdened young teacher share her story with us: all we human beings need is to be seen and heard for who we are. She unfolded right before us, revealing the hope at her core as she shared how she thought she had failed her students. Because we didn't judge her, she became freer to tell the truth. As she told the truth, she was free to see her strengths and not just her gaps in knowledge. She noticed where she was and shared her story in awe of being heard. Each of us had noticed where we were and witnessed a tiny but powerful moment of freedom.

Every day we are engaged in a miracle which we don't even recognize: a blue sky, white clouds, green leaves, the black, curious eyes of a child—our own two eyes. All is a miracle.
—Thich Nhat Hanh

This practice isn't easy for busy educators. Our minds are crammed with thoughts. Our lives are crammed with demands. Who has time to meditate, even though we know how beneficial meditation is to our well-being and our blood pressure? That's why these moments of appreciation make such a difference. We get to experience what matters and to see little miracles unfold.

Worry never robs tomorrow of its sorrow; it only saps today of its strength.
—A. J. Cronin

I call this process of noticing where we are "meditation in a moment" (MIM). Truth be told, this is the way I meditate. Perhaps I am moved by a piece of music or the quality of light as it streams through my window. Perhaps a child's shy smile calls to me or my beloved pup, Toby Grapelli, sits in front of me with his sweet, wild brown eyes, waiting for me to shower love on him. That's all it takes: one movement, one view, one wet-nosed nudge, one moment in gratitude.

That's my meditation. Each MIM gives me joy to pass along. Some people would label me a daydreamer. I am enrapt as in a dream. But there's nothing imaginary or unreal in my moments of meditation. In fact, the world feels more real to me than it did in the moment before I stopped to notice where I am.

Our Brains in the Quiet Moments

Nothing happens by accident. A moment of gratitude like a MIM soothes not just our spirits but our brain functioning as well. Nested in different nooks and crannies in this book, you will discover research insights streaming from the new field of neuroscience. This research offers us new understanding of the power of second chances. And the key to recognizing those second chances is to walk consciously through as many moments as we can each day, taking time to feel each step. Let's consider how neuroscientists can help us understand how our brains embrace or shove away a second chance.

Are our brains hardwired to allow for and even foster second chances? So much depends on the interplay between two neuro-centers in our brains: the amygdala and the prefrontal cortex. The amygdala, a small tight collection of four almond-shaped glands centrally located in our heads, constantly scans our surroundings for signs of danger. The prefrontal cortex, the parallel and moderating part of our brains, is also called our executive function.

Think of what an executive does: makes tough decisions, plans for the future, reads the story behind the story, sets priorities, keeps perspective, resolves conflicts, reasons things out, inspires and uplifts, and helps us laugh again. These are the everyday executive tasks performed by the prefrontal cortex. The prefrontal cortex can modulate, temper, and calm the amygdala. When the amygdala eschews change, the prefrontal cortex adapts to the challenge. We have choices about which part of our brains win the day. Over time, in little comforting ways, we can lean more toward calm than frenzy in the moment.

Picture how a quiet moment affects your brain. Do you know that serene feeling when your worries take a vacation, no matter how briefly? The scanning-for-danger amygdala may have done its job of delivering you alert into a quiet moment. Your breathing calms. Your heart slows, and now it's time for the amygdala's partner and sometimes ally, the prefrontal cortex, to step in. At the Ranthambore National Park, a large tiger reserve in northern India, our hearts pounded when we spotted tiger footprints but slowed to an awestruck meditation as we watched the tiger pad his way beneath the trees.

Your prefrontal cortex restfully waits for you to take a breath and stop your busy ways just for a moment. Your amygdala and prefrontal cortex are about to shake hands in support of one another. In this moment, you are alert but not afraid, in awe but not overwhelmed. You are alert enough to notice where you are in the moment and serene enough to enjoy what has captured your attention. I finally had witnessed firsthand the wonder of William Blake's poem: "Tiger, tiger, burning bright / In the forests of the night, / What immortal hand or eye / Could frame thy fearful symmetry?"

This state of internal lyrical harmony happens when your systems are working together. By stepping back and inviting this peaceful island into our lives, we take a mini-vacation from our worries. By inviting and welcoming this harmony over and over again, we begin to feel as if serenity is second nature to us. In this harmonious state, our readiness to see and act on second chances grows. By meditating in the moment, we position ourselves to find inspiration in the ordinary and joy in the everyday. This is the comfort of little things.

Finding Those Quiet Moments through Meditation

You may well have your own preferred way to meditate. For someone like me with a busy mind, I have trouble with seated meditation: My mind wanders. However, by "noticing where I am" in the moment, I feel the same quiet peacefulness and sense of gratitude I feel when I am able to get into a sitting (or walking) meditation.

Workplace studies show conclusively that meditation increases our physical well-being as much as it renews our positive attitude. In "Meditating at Work: A New Approach to Managing Overload," Wendy Woods (2012) points to two studies that support this claim. In one study, those who participated in an eight-week Mindfulness Based Stress Reduction (MBSR) program, which included a daily meditation lasting an average of twenty-seven minutes, experienced increased activity in their left prefrontal cortex—the region of the brain that is home to positive emotions and constructive problem solving. In another study, involving nurses, even ten minutes of meditation five times per week for one month lowered "symptoms of burnout, enhancing relaxation, and improving life satisfaction."

Do you know of any educator, including yourself, who wouldn't welcome enhanced relaxation and increased life satisfaction? Yet, just as many colleagues as there have been studies tell me, "I don't have time to meditate," or "I've tried but I can't meditate." Guess what? Notice where you are in the moment. Take a MIM break and you are meditating. Check your heart rate. Your steadiness may surprise you. As the bumper sticker reminds us, "Meditation: It's not what you think it is."

Meditation doesn't have to be conducted from a seated position or even outside of everyday events. Holding to a strict definition of meditation can be off-putting: How on earth can I claim a quiet space and time to meditate, and even if I could, how can I quiet down the chattering committee in my head?

A MIM frees us from that box. A MIM invoked by awe in the moment literally stops us in our tracks. MIMs come as naturally as a toddler's hug or as preternaturally as seeing a tiger stride out of the jungle beside you. Our task is to stop, pay attention, breathe, and enjoy. If it feels right, express gratitude for having your eyes and heart opened to magic. Gratitude extends the impact of a MIM.

Give Yourself a Break

Give yourself this moment to take a look around you (step outside, observe a child, notice something beautiful to you). What calls your attention? Pay attention to that. Watch. Listen. Appreciate. Allow yourself to marvel.

Being in the Moment

Can't sit still long enough to meditate? I empathize. Trust me; my mind boomerangs like popcorn in a hot popcorn popper when I try to sit still and let go of those thoughts.

But meditation comes in many forms, and not all of these forms require lengthy sitting. Walking mindfully is another form of meditating. Daily I walk the neighborhoods of my old—but new to me—New England mill town, looking up for an architectural whimsy: a duck-shaped wind vane or perhaps an unexpected stained glass entryway. Notice where you are in the moment, whether you are moving or holding still, and you are meditating. Just notice where you are. Check your heart rate. Your steadiness may surprise you.

Awe Is a Pathway to Second Chances

When is the last time you were awestruck? Were you taken by something a child said or something you read? Our challenge as educators is to allow ourselves to live in those moments. Don't run. Don't hide. Just be there to witness what you can, and let yourself enjoy the mystery. If this sounds too pie-in-the-sky unrealistic, consider the following study: Zoë Chance, a guest on my radio program, *Heart to Heart Conversations on Leadership: Your Guide to Making a Difference*, explains that researchers are onto the value of brief, passing moments of awe. Chance says research shows that we feel less pressured and that we have more time than we actually do (by the clock) when we are transfixed in the moment.

To help employees of corporations experience these restorative moments, managers establish video-playing rooms where employees can sit briefly and watch a snippet of a film like Jimmy Stewart's eureka moment in *It's a Wonderful Life*. Employees walk out of the darkness with more light in their eyes.

To listen to my conversation with Zoë Chance, "Too Little Time?: Find More Time in Unexpected Place," go to www.bamradionetwork.com and type "Zoë Chance" into the search box.

*Comfort in
Little Things*

What is your favorite
quotation, poem, or
saying? Create and
place a copy of those
words where you will
see them daily. Take
a moment to read the
quote or say it aloud to
yourself. If one word
or phrase calls out
to you, read it aloud
again. Allow the words
and their meaning to
soothe your soul.

A similar moment of awe just fell into my pathway. As I stepped off my plane from Boston into Washington National airport, I walked into a vision: soldiers in dress uniform, little children with Sunday-best outfits waving flags, and a brass band playing Duke Ellington's "It Don't Mean a Thing (If It Ain't Got That Swing)." An Honor Flight of World War II soldiers was about to arrive from upstate New York.

I dropped my bags and joined the gratitude line of applauding and whistling travelers happy to honor the soldiers who were never fully honored. Beside me stood a Vietnam vet from Florida who had come to witness the moment. As the white-haired men and women emerged in wheelchairs, supported by canes or under their own steam, we went wild! Soldiers saluted soldiers. Cameras clicked. Dazzled children waved flags.

And I? As I looked into the eyes of 103-year-old Marine veteran Betty, I flew to her to give her a hug and big kiss, saying, "Thank you, bless you, you opened the doors for all of us who follow." Betty grasped my hand, looked me squarely in the eye, and said: "Yes, we paved the way."

When veteran Mr. Schwartz got his hug and kiss he said, "Don't know what my wife will say, but honey, you made my day!" A moment of awe not only makes a day brilliant, a moment of awe finds a home in our hearts.

Being with all the vets I met that day riveted me in the moment. I was awestruck, entranced, joyously grateful. The Honor Flight moment crackled with second chances, not just for the soldiers who deserved it most, but for those of us who welcomed them home. Second chances like this lead each of us home: home is the loving place where we know what matters and where we rest easy.

I feel so blessed that I was in the right place at the right time. I know, however, that finding a second chance involves more than that. I needed to say, "Let me be here. Let me be present. Let me honor each of these heroes. Let my heart be open." That's all it took. Call it a MIM, a blessing, or pure happenstance: If you allow yourself to be awestruck by the beauty of the moment, your life will change. Your second chance from the outside will become your second chance for your inside.

Margaret Jones, reader of the blog, shares her story of second chances:

I am learning to face my fears with wonder rather than hope. When my confidence is waning, I look for the note on my desk that reminds me to "wonder how welcoming surprise might change my way of teaching." Hope leaves the door open for disappointment if my expectations are not met. Wonder leaves the door open for whatever life might have in store for me.

—Margaret Jones, September 29, 2014

The experience of eternity right here and now is the function of life. Heaven is not the place to have the experience; here is the place to have the experience.

—Joseph Campbell

Here's the spiritual principle: Notice the beauty that calls out to you, including the beauty within each person you see. Notice that. Accept that. Hold still to appreciate that. Offer that to others. Your second chances will shower themselves like shooting stars in your heaven. You may even see something of beauty in yourself that you had not allowed yourself to notice before. Why not invite the magnificence of the Perseid meteor shower season to light up your insides?

Reflection Questions

1. What sparks awe in you? Can you recall the last time you were awestruck? What was beneath the surface during the moment that spoke to your heart? What did you need to hear that you heard loud and clear in that moment?

2. Do you know an unsung hero who deserves to be honored? Most of the educators I know are unsung heroes, doing their job and making a difference in unnoticed moments (unnoticed by others perhaps, but remembered always by the child or family member we touched). What could you do to honor that person, anonymously or publicly? You have the power to create moments of awe. What will you do to make that happen?

3. Does "traditional" meditation work for you? Are you able to sit still and meditate? If so, can or have you found a way to incorporate this practice into your day so you feel restored? In fact, how might your practice of meditation give you a second chance at appreciating what you have?

4. If you are like me and traditional meditation is a challenge, where do you need to go to find inspiration?

5. What piece of music uplifts you? Who inspires you? Where on earth can you go where you will feel awestruck?

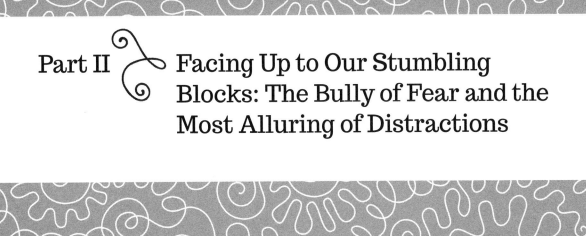

Part II — Facing Up to Our Stumbling Blocks: The Bully of Fear and the Most Alluring of Distractions

Chapter 4

Squaring Off against the Bully of Fear

You gain strength, courage, and confidence by every experience
in which you really stop to look fear in the face. . . . You must do the thing
you think you cannot do.—*Eleanor Roosevelt*

What Eleanor Knew

I know when my self-confidence abandons me. I'm not always sure how self-doubt seeps in, but I am sure of the result: Work that felt so natural and so easy overwhelms me. When self-doubt takes over, a simple twenty-minute task festoons into a full-day's labor.

Perhaps you know how this goes. Even a promising long-awaited adventure like a midsummer's day at the lake collapses into a heavy burden.

As I made the two-hour drive to Vermont to swim at my favorite crystalline lake with the hidden access through the woods, little worries began shooting darts through my joy. By the time I had parked my car to begin my hike down and up the circuitous, pine-forested hillside path to the water's edge, clouds had elbowed out the sun.

"My" lake had become a stranger. Its once welcoming water felt cold to the touch and precipitously deep. Chop edged out placidity as the concerns inside me spread outside. And so, I stood at water's edge of the clear lake

I have always loved, poised to dive but scared. How could I plunge into a possible choking panic attack or a disabling leg cramp?

Catching on that the Bully of Fear was stalking me from within, I breathed in, closed my eyes, breathed out, and asked for help. At times like this, the kindest thing I can do for myself is to surrender my illusion of control, ask for help, and wait.

As I waited and as I breathed, I recalled an image of Eleanor Roosevelt's smilingly bold and determined countenance from the Ken Burns documentary *The Roosevelts: An Intimate History* (2014). And I remembered that Eleanor knew hard times. I recalled what she knew:

- Eleanor knew that when her heart ached, she needed to walk steadily toward and into the bathroom: to close the door securely behind her, to lock the door, and to turn the sink's hot and cold water spigots to full blast. Shielded by the gushing sound, Eleanor could allow herself to cry: "Every time you meet a situation, though you may think at the time it is an impossibility and you go through the tortures of the damned, once you have met it and lived through it, you find that forever after you are freer than you were before." (1960, 29)

- Eleanor knew how it felt when her trusted personal secretary and the husband she adored betrayed her and became lovers. Eleanor knew that even with a broken heart, she could still claim personal dignity: "The giving of love is an education in itself."

- Eleanor knew how to comfort hospitalized war-ravaged soldiers, regardless of her terror as their shell-shocked, careening minds veered off the edge of sanity and their wounds refused to heal: "We do not have to become heroes overnight. Just a step at a time, meeting each thing that comes up, seeing it as not as dreadful as it appeared, discovering we have the strength to stare it down." (1960, 41)

- Eleanor knew that her looks would not open doors and that the world she lived in was not necessarily open to a bright and questioning woman. "As for accomplishments, I just did what I had to do as things came along. A stumbling block to the pessimist is a stepping-stone to the optimist."

- Eleanor knew the risks as she steadfastly took action for civil rights, despite death threats from the Ku Klux Klan: "Staying aloof is not a solution, but a cowardly evasion." (1963, 19)

- Eleanor, knowing and experiencing all of these losses and threats, kept weaving tragedy into wisdom: "You gain strength, courage, and confidence by every experience in which you really stop to look fear in the face. . . . You must do the thing you think you cannot do." (1960, 29)

- Eleanor knew: "In the long run, we shape our lives, and we shape ourselves. The process never ends until we die. And the choices we make are ultimately our own responsibility." (1960, p. x) Eleanor Roosevelt reinvented herself several times. As she reinvented herself, she fully accepted the second chances that came her way. She created second chances when none was offered.

Eleanor knew what I am still learning:

- Confidence grows, and confidence wanes.

- As often as you can, kick fear to the curb, no matter how terrifying the circumstances.

- Choose to love and to grow, regardless of having no guarantees.

- Choose to be true to your dream, against all odds. In so doing, inspire others to trust in their dreams.

When you can, look fear in the face. Not every second chance to reclaim joy or hope or confidence comes easily. The choice, no matter how clouded over, is always there. What second chances await you even on low-confidence, wearisome days?

That day at the lake, I left my red sandals at the water's edge just before I said, "What the hey?" and dove into the water in the sometimes sun.

Amygdala Hijack, a.k.a. the Bully of Fear

In moments of self-doubt, we are especially vulnerable to what Daniel Goleman calls an "amygdala hijack" (1995). When the amygdala gland takes control of our body, we lose our ability to think straight, causing heart-pounding enzymes like adrenaline and cortisol to course through our system. Perspective flies out the nearest window. All it takes to trigger a hijack is one last-straw event or comment that throws us into an out-of-control swirl of emotions.

In this state, when we are red faced and spoiling for an attack, we are in danger of doing or saying things we will later regret. We remove ourselves from the realm of accepting or giving second chances. A two-year-old chomps down on a classmate's shoulder. A teacher screams at a roughhousing child. A director leaps over the steps of progressive discipline and proclaims to a challenging employee: "You're fired!" Consequences of allowing our amygdala to control us often come back to haunt us.

Have you known someone who gets a mad on for days? That person may go to bed reliving the upsetting event and wake up angry the next morning, and the following night, and the following morning. The amygdala's function is to keep us alert so we can protect ourselves from threats. By recalling the threat or the injustice or the slight over and over again, we keep the adrenaline (or cortisol) coursing through our body.

Amygdala hijacks can last for seconds or for weeks. My mother called this dynamic of keeping our emotions roiling and boiling "licking your wounds." My father would exhort, "Rise above it!" Sayings like "licking your wounds," "throw salt on your wounds," "rise above it," "pushing your buttons," and "getting under your skin" are all homespun ways of describing our daily relationship with our amygdala.

Amygdala Hijacks and Gender

Gender may play a role in how we respond to amygdala hijacks. Little boys in particular have an ability to get angry and get over it (Chesler 2009) Their storm cloud passes as hurriedly as it appears. Little girls learn early on to take less direct approaches to their anger. Hence, few of us are surprised to hear that four-year-old girls are already forming exclusive cliques. Cliques protect girls from threats they perceive from outsiders, providing the "strength in numbers" temporary solution to a deeper problem: exclusion (Starr 2005). When either children or adults are overtaken by an amygdala hijack, they shut out the possibility of second chances.

Squaring Off against the Bully: Regaining Dignity

When the amygdala takes over, how do we begin to find our way back to calm? How can we get free enough to be awestruck or to notice the beauty within and around us? How on earth, for example, is Lyra, whom we met in chapter 2, ever going to regain serenity? Little Winston was injured on her watch, precisely because she wasn't watching. How are you going to find peace when you know you have so many demands waiting at your door?

Beverlyn Cain offers one option. In response to my post number six, "Untying Myself," on my blog *Share Your Stories*, she describes how she manages her amygdala into productivity, finding beauty in what could have been a beastly experience. Cain channels high anxiety into "positive energy":

Another view is getting past a "post-traumatic stress" situation from a past issue that causes high anxiety whenever a new situation appears to look like it may go in that direction. From personal experience, I work on taking charge. So as Holly suggests, deal with the present situation in a productive manner. Sit on the anxiety, power walk, do yoga, something to bring myself to a balanced calm mind-set. The reality is that I either have the choice of wallowing in negative energy, which gets me nowhere, or assertively handling the situation, which exudes positive energy.

—Beverlyn Cain, June 4, 2014

Tools to Use against the Bully

Acknowledging that the Bully of Fear is always at the ready to pester us, we can educate ourselves without huge effort on how to prevent our buttons from getting pushed and how to defuse the buttons when pushed. You already have some of these skills inside you. Do you breathe calmly, for example, when someone is getting under your skin? Do you silently repeat your favorite saying, like "This too shall pass"?

Let's break this down one step at a time by looking first at what pushes our buttons and second at little comforting actions we can take to restore our dignity. As we restore our dignity, we increase the likelihood of our being open to second chances.

What Pushes Your Buttons?

Take a moment to mentally list, type, write, or share with a trusted colleague/friend: What adult behaviors push your buttons? For sure, children's behavior can also get under our skin. Usually a child who whines is tired; a child who cries needs to be soothed. A child who acts out needs our full attention. For a helpful resource on preventing our buttons from being pushed by children, see *Social Emotional Tools for Life* (Forrester and Albrecht 2014). You'll find strategies that work in the moment and are also preventative.

Your Ounce of Prevention

1. List at least three behaviors that push your buttons.
2. Identify at least three ways to prevent these behaviors from overtaking you.

When I ask educators what child behaviors push their buttons, here's what they say:

- whining
- negativity
- "attitude"
- entitlement
- not taking responsibility
- resistance to changing for the better

- gossiping, stirring up trouble
- being disrespectful
- dishonesty

My list also includes being:

- manipulative,
- indirect,
- condescending, and
- snarky (hurtfully sarcastic or flippant).

We tend to be more understanding and less reactive when children push our buttons; after all, we are the adult in the room. What really gets under our skin is the adult whose behavior pushes our buttons.

Let's put button pushers in perspective. Here are some common ones in many professions:

- disrespect
- being treated unfairly or arbitrarily
- not being heard or seen
- aggression (bullying)
- being held to unrealistic deadlines

Congratulations! By making your own list of button-pushing behaviors and by reading about what pushes the buttons of other educators, you have taken a valuable step in preventing and managing an amygdala hijack. Knowledge is powerful. Now that you have acknowledged what bothers you, you are in a better position to ward off those behaviors. As my colleague Ann Terrell reminds me, "When you see crazy coming down your side of the street, cross the street."

You'll be better able to see the button-pushers coming your way.

If the Bully of Fear creeps up on you without your noticing, you can now identify how to diffuse the Bully's effect and regain your professionalism.

Preventing or Diffusing the Power of the Bully of Fear

Let's start with what you know. You have ways of keeping your cool when you are stressed. You have ways of preventing people from pushing your buttons. You already have ways to call on your executive function.

Let's identify what you do to keep your equilibrium when people or things bother you. The goal is to acknowledge, give credit to, and build on appropriate practices.

- What's your go-to approach to stay calm and carry on?
- If you can't use your favored approach, what else have you done?
- What have you witnessed another person do while stressed that you might want to emulate?

If you said you walk away, breathe, count to ten, or say a prayer, you are in line with what most educators tell me. Below is the list I have compiled over the years from my own experience and from researching the topic of what helps us prevent a full-blown amygdala hijack.

You can do the following without having to leave the situation:

- Memorize, recall, and recite your favorite saying or verse, for example, "This too shall pass."
- Sing a song to yourself that restores you, silently if necessary.
- Play your favorite music "in your head"; Brahms is my man, although Duke Ellington at the piano also works.
- Breathe intentionally. Start in your belly. Expand your chest. Open your throat. Now, just as deliberately, blow out the used air from your throat, chest, and finally your belly. Do this again.
- Rotate your shoulders back. Again.
- Repeat to yourself: "It's not about me." Taking stress personally amps up the amygdala.
- Picture the person who is stressing you out in her underwear. This was Lucille Ball's technique.

- Do something (constructive) with your hands, such as straightening the paper piles on your desk.
- Blow bubbles. Watch them as they float and cavort.
- Count to ten. Count backwards from ten.
- Picture yourself somewhere safe and soothing.
- Remind yourself of the message of your favorite children's book.
- Add any other steps you take here:

_____

_____

If you need to leave the scene, you can do the following:

- Walk away.
- Visit the infant room; rock a baby.
- Call or text an understanding friend.
- Step outside (or at least look out the window).
- Listen to music on your iPod.
- Bust a move.
- Make human contact: Ask for a hug (shake a hand), or just sit with a safe person.
- Alternately, if you require solitariness, claim a bathroom stall as your temporary office.
- Bring a therapy dog to work. Or a cat. Or a fish.
- Eat fruit to reintroduce healthy sucrose to your system.
- Add any other steps you take that help you get out from under a threat here:

_____

_____

Each technique is a step toward defusing the ticking-bomb amygdala.

When you take steps to de-stress, you literally flip the switch on your internal systems. This begins in the amygdala's zone, the more primitive unconscious autonomic system. The autonomic system governs these body functions:

- heart rate
- digestion
- breathing
- swallowing
- pupil dilation

As soon as you step back, you call upon the more sophisticated system, the central nervous system which governs these functions:

- conscious thought: translation of impulses into quantifiable thoughts and feelings
- decision making
- modulation of the fight, flight, or freeze response
- well-being
- higher functions including optimism, humor, and spirituality

The essential effect of whichever brain system is in charge is that we act intentionally or unconsciously. Professionalism is acting consciously while trusting our gut reaction and, more importantly, how we interpret our gut instinct.

Which of these approaches might you recommend to preschool director Yalena in the case study below? Far more second chances await Yalena than she at first imagines. You know how it goes when someone knocks you off base: threats appear to rob us of choices. Let's challenge that expectation.

CASE STUDY *Director Yalena's Nemesis, Preschool Teacher Trixie Marie*

Trixie Marie, a preschool teacher, is Yalena's worst nightmare. Trixie Marie has always believed she would be the best leader for the Happy Valley Child Care. But she refuses to take the course work to be qualified as a director. But that's okay with Trixie Marie; she doesn't need the money. She always says her family's funeral home will never go out of business.

Happy Valley's longest-term employee, Trixie Marie has witnessed directors come and directors go. And she is proud that she has played no small part in getting rid of most of the directors. Trixie Marie is currently "spoiling for" the new director, Yalena.

Trixie Marie knows just what to do: Pretend to support Yalena. Volunteer to ease Yalena's burdens. Act as if she is Yalena's best friend. Share secrets about other staff while saying, "Don't tell anybody I told you this." Smile at Yalena while using just the right words to get under Yalena's skin:

- "Yalena, that new dress is gorgeous on you. You must have lost some of those extra pounds."

- "Don't worry about Terrence coming in late again; I've already warned him that you are going to write him up. Of course, he threatened to sue you for sex discrimination. Can you believe that man?"

- "Tariq's mom asked if she can pick up Tariq after we close tonight: I told her you would not allow any such thing, even if she has an emergency. Some parents should not be allowed to have children!"

- "Did I mention that the chair of our board is my daughter's godfather? Oh yes, we go way back! He and I had a very interesting conversation last night at the country club. Oh, and guess who else I saw there at the bar *again*?"

- "Of course I'll have my classroom portfolio in to you on time. I just need you to show me one more time how you want me to do that documentation."

Trixie Marie reminds Yalena of Yalena's best friend in high school, Jessica—the one who stole Yalena's boyfriend, Moses! Yalena wants to scream every time Yalena sees Trixie Marie's fake, sugary smile. Yalena fears, however, that getting on the wrong side of Trixie Marie will offend Trixie Marie's clique on the staff. Yalena never likes to confront staff anyway; she believes that modeling the right thing to do will encourage staff to change.

What would you advise Yalena to do to prevent an amygdala hijack thanks to Trixie Marie's hijinks? In fact, can you envision any way in which this conflict can be liberating for Yalena, and maybe even Trixie Marie? Each of these educators can make the choice to either stay stuck or take a second chance.

Applying the Tools: Helping Director Yalena

Consider asking Yalena the following questions to help her through this dilemma:

1. Name the adult behaviors that push your buttons.
2. Which of these behaviors did Trixie Marie exhibit at the staff meeting?
3. What helps you keep your cool when you see trouble coming your way?
4. If your buttons get pushed, what tools do you use to calm down and regain a sense of professionalism?
5. Do you want to keep Trixie Marie on staff or help her out the door?
6. If you want to retain Trixie Marie, tell her clearly what behavior is acceptable and what is not; establish a corrective action plan to monitor her behaviors.
7. If you want to say good-bye to Trixie Marie, what do you need to document before you take her through the three steps of progressive discipline?
8. Does Trixie Marie remind you of anyone else? Can you separate that "old" relationship from your current issues with Trixie Marie?
9. Take a ten-minute break to walk outside or sit quietly in a space you love, taking time to "notice where you are" (see chapter 3 for more ideas on how to do this).
10. Keeping your eyes on the prize of doing what's best for children and families, what must you do to remedy this situation?

Second Chances in the Midst of Difficulty

When we are at our worst, we have the greatest opportunity. When we are most threatened, we can call upon our greatest tool of all: courage. When we feel hopeless or overwhelmed, we still have a choice. We can breathe, step back, and ask, as author Gus Lee advises us, "What's my highest possible moral act?" in this situation (Lee and Couras, "Do You Have the Courage to Be an Effective Educational Leader?"). What choice can I make that will make the biggest difference to children and families in the long run?

Looking up for even a moment to consider "the long run" points us on the path to our second chance. As we and Yalena choose courage, we inspire everyone around us to turn ugly moments into moments of clarity and liberation.

To help Yalena take a step-by-step process to hold resistant staff accountable, see *What You Need to Lead an Early Childhood Program* (Bruno 2012). To ensure that you are prepared to walk employees through the three steps of progressive discipline, you might also want to check out *Managing Legal Risks in Early Childhood Programs* (Bruno and Copeland 2012).

To listen to my conversation with Gus Lee, "Do You Have the Courage to Be an Effective Educational Leader?," go to www .bamradionetwork .com and type "Gus Lee" into the search box.

Partner with Your Brain

Brain science can add to our anti-bully strategy. Let's see how we can partner with our evolving brain to transcend the amygdala by embracing the amygdala. Just as human beings are complex, so is the human brain. Being able to see through the complexity helps us claim meaning in the mundane and freedom in restriction.

Beauty Tames Beast: How about That Prefrontal Cortex?

Place your hand over your forehead. If you are comfortable enough, close your eyes. Using your fingertips or the heel of your hand, gently massage or rub any place on your forehead that could use a healing touch. Be sure to massage that triangular space between your eyebrows and a little above.

You have just soothed the prefrontal cortex. It is the place on our heads where the newest part of our brain resides, directly behind the bones of our forehead. Our ancestors referred to this central area as our "third eye," which they believed was all-seeing. I call it "Beauty" because it partners so well with the more primitive "Beast," as the amygdala gland.

The amygdala (Beast) alerts, provokes, and calls out to the prefrontal cortex (Beauty): "Help me out here! I'm about to lose it!" Our executive function can get to work calming the amygdala even as adrenaline floods our system, sweeping wisdom down the drain in the process. The prefrontal cortex reassures the amygdala: "I'm here. We'll get through this together. Each time we work together, things get easier. Breathe. Now, let's get to work."

To listen to my conversation with Louis Cozolino, "3 Keys to Leading People Who Push Your Buttons," go to www .bamradionetwork .com, and type "Louis Cozolino" into the search box.

Maturity grows as we learn to shift from the provocation of the moment to the possibility of the moment. There's magic in this next fact: As we mature, the more we call upon our prefrontal cortex to partner with, learn from, and calm the amygdala's urgency, the easier and more instinctual this soothing process becomes. According to Louis Cozolino, "as we get older, the amygdala continues to work just as well at some of its jobs—in other words, recognizing and analyzing facial expressions and things like that— but it seems much less activated by fear and anxiety" (Cozolino, "3 Keys to Leading People Who Push Your Buttons").

Our brain is constructed to help us become older and wiser. Stressors don't have to ignite explosions. Stressors can spark insights. Responsibilities don't have to burden us; responsibilities can give our lives meaning. Fear doesn't have to overwhelm us. Fear lets us know that change is in the wind. Anger empowers us to act but to act wisely.

Raw reactions transition to reflective reaction. Intelligent responses transform into wise decisions. Beast eases up. Beauty accepts Beast as a gift. Beast and Beauty boogie through the dark night into the promise of dawn. What initially pushed our buttons can deliver us to the place where we can step back, observe, and choose to act wisely. At the Ranthambore National Park in India, we were all anxious about what might emerge from the jungle; however, our alertness helped us spot and be awestruck by the strolling tiger. Did I mention that our guide told us the tiger had eaten his fill recently? Sometimes awe needs a practical nudge.

Get Real: How Can I Befriend What Bothers Me the Most?

How on earth do we befriend the amygdala and tame it to partner with the prefrontal cortex? For years, humans have asked, how do we soothe the savage beast? How do we rise above the conflict to find enduring answers? Reclaiming our birthright to joy is the goal, but is this easier said than done for overcommitted educators? Not if we take the process one breath at a time.

Uniting Steps and Strategies

Following these steps will consolidate your skill to build a partnership between your hotheaded amygdala and your strong, true voice within:

1. Acknowledge when a threat is hovering.
2. Identify what you need in the moment.
3. Find safety by stepping out of the tornado's direct pathway and accepting and transforming the tornado's energy.
4. Give yourself a second chance to be inspired.
5. Pass that gift onto others.

One additional thought might also help you reclaim your professionalism: Be aware of the possibility that past, unresolved conflicts can intensify amygdala hijacks. This final principle offers perspective on why some conflicts may feel unresolvable.

Be Mindful of Overlays

We have talked about what steals our serenity, what hijacks our amygdala, and what shuts off the blood flow to the more mature part of our brain. Now let's kick it up a notch. Let's look at one of the most troublesome dynamics that interferes with making mature, professional decisions.

I call this "dynamic overlay." Overlay occurs when we allow past unresolved conflicts to sabotage our willingness and our capacity to resolve today's issue. We literally paint over today's situation with the dark colors of past conflicts. As we overlay, we obscure and sometimes obliterate our vision. We can't see the problem for what it is. The problem becomes instead a holy war that we must win to reclaim our esteem and dignity.

We all experience this dynamic, but some of us experience it more intensely than others. We can all work to remain in the moment, noticing where we are rather than allowing ourselves to be whipped around by old concerns. We have choices. Choices give us second chances. By making the choice to distinguish a past hurt from a present conflict, we are able to see the current situation for what it is: a problem to be resolved.

As a person who has post-traumatic stress disorder from childhood violence and neglect, I call upon a professional counselor to help me separate the past from the present. Over time, however, I have become better able to sense when I am sabotaging myself with overlay. The energy is different when I load a past hurt onto a present issue. As Twelve-Step colleagues remind me, "If you're hysterical, it's historical!"

You know you are overlaying the unresolved past on the present when you "climb up on your high horse" and feel as if you are better than the other person. You "take the moral high ground" where your dignity cannot be assailed. You feel righteously indignant.

An everyday resolvable conflict turns into an epic battle for truth, justice, and the American way. You are 800 percent certain you are in the right. If others can't see the world as you see it, they need to get over themselves. When you start feeling this way, it's time to work toward alleviating the hurt from the past. Until that injustice has been remedied, the holy war will rage on.

Our amygdala thrives on overlay. With the amygdala's help, overlay keeps us roiled up and hopping indignant. We know we are right. And we *are* right. No one should have perpetrated that injustice upon you, and no one has the right to tell you not to feel as upset as you do. Nonetheless, roiled up as we are, our executive function doesn't stand a chance. We are too stuck in the past to notice where we are in the present.

As you read my story below, ask yourself, does this remind me of anything I have experienced? And how might preschool director Yalena apply what I learned to her situation?

 *Untying Myself*

This dollar-store twine circling my left wrist is knotted into a rough bracelet. Why would I, lover of sea-glass green and luminescent opal, bother with a fading and frumpy beige adornment?

Good question.

If you have a trusted friend who reminds you to get over yourself and move on, you know how my twine bracelet helps me.

Do you, as I do, have a knack for:

- getting in your own way?
- making a decision more complicated than it needs to be?
- overthinking simple situations?

Because I am expert at all of these practices, I tie myself up in knots. Unnecessary knots. Touching my rough, knotted bracelet reminds me that just as I tied the knots, I can untie the knots.

May I tell you about one of my familiar knots; how I tie it; and how, with conscious effort, I can untie it?

Despite my "what the hey?" attitude, my feelings can be easily hurt. Recently I was presenting a workshop with two colleagues. We each had an allotted time. I went over my designated time. I get so exuberant I lose track of time; for that reason, I ask my colleagues to signal me when I need to wrap up. I did not see a signal.

My colleague who spoke after me stated her displeasure twice at having less than her designated time. Yes, I went over time. But I counted on her to let me know when I needed to end. Publicly embarrassed, I wilted in a shame attack followed by feeling betrayed.

Looking back, I see this was a simple miscommunication of expectations. I expected a signal from my colleague, and she expected me to know when to end.

When I feel shamed in public, alarms blare. Outwardly, I put on a professional face; inwardly, I beat myself up and want to run away. My colleagues had no idea!

That's where the knot comes in: I was overlaying past, painful memories on a current event and returning to a time when I was all of sixteen years old.

Comfort in Little Things

Find something tactile and sensory to hold in your hand that soothes you: perhaps a small, smooth river rock; your grandmother's soft, old-fashioned handkerchief; or muted beach glass. Carry this "talisman" with you and hold it when you need to be grounded. Or carry a **Q-Tip** to remind yourself: "Quit taking it personally."

My father, bless him, announced in front of others that I was not intelligent enough to win scholarships to universities. His pronouncement wounded me. My confidence crumpled for days before I could rebound with silent "I am not stupid!" conviction. Soon after, I took the competitive New York State Regents Examination and won a scholarship. But rebuilding my self-esteem is a lifelong project.

When my colleague intimated to the audience that I was wrong, she was right. However, I felt publicly shamed—again. That public shaming shoved me back into a well of unworthiness. She became a demeaning parent, and I, the kicked-to-the-curb child. The result was knots in my heart, knots in the room, and a potential knot in our relationship.

One touch to my bracelet reminded me that I created this knot. My colleagues had no clue. I was blaming them for the pain of my childhood. I was expecting them to make the past pain right.

"If you're hysterical, the problem is historical," my Twelve-Step groups remind me.

My shame attack was not caused by my colleagues, nor were they responsible for fixing me!

Overlaying past unresolved conflict on today's misunderstanding does not resolve anything. When I take this path, I feel righteous indignation. I stand on the moral high ground. I surrender my maturity. I lose sight of the present.

Hello?

The truth is that each time a wound is reopened, I am given a second chance to heal. I don't have to turn a simple misconnection into drama. I can separate past from present.

This joint presentation was a simple problem with a simple solution. I apologized to my colleagues, requested a definite way of signaling one another about time boundaries in the future, and offered to go last the next time we present.

I reminded myself that I have a choice: I can choose to live in the present, deal directly with the present misunderstanding, take responsibility for my part in the misunderstanding, learn, and let go.

I'll take that second chance.

—Holly Elissa, May 29, 2014

Curing Overlay: Another Practical Example

How do you feel about going to the dentist? Today, my dental checkups and six-month cleanings are routine. I know the life story of my dental hygienist and can name each grandchild in the pictures that hang in her office. I joke amiably with Dr. Scherr.

If I have to have serious work done, like a root canal, I make an appointment right away to see the orthodontist, who understands panic disorder. She offers me *I Love Lucy* videos, gives full and clear explanations of the procedure, checks in with me frequently to get a thumbs-up or -down on how I am doing, and tells me how much time we have left in each stage of the root canal.

If I need it, I take medication. I'm okay with that. A diabetic takes insulin to even out his system. A trauma survivor takes calming medication to prevent a panic attack (which is a huge amygdala hijack). I leave unevenly smiling, knowing I have been and will be okay. I have faced another conflict without the oppression of overlay. With each root canal, I grow more confident that all will be well.

I didn't always have this level of comfort with dental work. In my early twenties, I avoided dental visits as often as I could. I had excuses. I was moving. I was in a new community. I didn't have a "regular" dentist. I didn't have the money. I became an excuse-making machine.

When a tooth was inflamed and I could no longer kid myself with excuses, I was terrified. I had to force myself to find a dentist, call the dentist, make my appointment with the dentist, get myself to the appointment, and walk through the door of his office, all without turning right back around and running out the same door.

The new dentist turned out to be good enough once I got in his office. He did one thing differently than Dr. Tunney, the dentist of my childhood. My new dentist used something called novocaine. Oh my. The once-jarring sound of the drill no longer meant unbearable pain. My open mouth no longer endured torture. I was hysterical because the problem was historical. As was the practice of the time, Dr. Tunney used no novocaine, and he refused to let parents sit with their children in his office. Those feelings of terror in the presence of my new dentist? Pure overlay. The new dentist was not Dr. Tunney, and I was not a terrified child. If I hadn't taken the time to work my way through the overlay, I might be wearing dentures today!

Give Yourself a Break

You know that adult behavior that drives you crazy? Picture yourself effectively choosing and using one tool to maintain your serenity "when you see crazy walking down the street in your direction." Remember: "It's not about you."

Overlay is common in early childhood programs. We don't like conflict. Many of us prefer to believe underperforming staff will magically improve without being confronted. How often have we heard, "You've got to change who I work with. She and I have a personality conflict. We can't work together. End of story"?

Imagine how much easier it would be to resolve our conflicts if we were able to separate our past troubles from our present work challenges! Remember Yalena? She needed to confront Trixie Marie about her unprofessional behaviors. But Yalena is stuck in the past, remembering her high school "friend" who betrayed Yalena by moving in on her boyfriend. If Yalena allows the same well of anger to gush over onto her relationship with Trixie Marie, all kinds of inappropriate things might happen. Normally calm Yalena might yell. She might cry. Or she might fail to follow program procedures. If Yalena doesn't acknowledge the overlay, she will not be able to see the conflict with Trixie Marie for what it is: a work situation that needs to be addressed immediately and professionally. The calm executive function must prevail over the excitable amygdala.

Not sure if overlay is at play? Ask yourself these questions:

- Am I unduly shaken or emotional about this conflict?
- Is my anger or fear out of proportion to the situation at hand?
- What am I afraid might happen if I take action?
- Am I trying to right a past wrong, or am I addressing this specific challenge that I face today?
- Would I benefit from the help of a skilled counselor so I can learn from the past and live more in the present?

Managing and Moving On from Overlay

By now you know the drill: use your amygdala's infusion of energy while calling upon the wisdom of your prefrontal cortex. Of course your buttons are pushed. But now you know which behaviors push your buttons. You also have practices in place that allow you to step to the side so that buttons can't be pushed. Be as honest with yourself as you can: What would it take for you to face the conflict "as is," without the overlay of so much history you'll never get through it?

Here are tips on how to manage and move on from overlay. Ask yourself the following questions:

- How intense are my feelings (fear? anger? resentment?) about this conflict?
- Am I in a "If you're hysterical, it must be historical" state?
- Do I feel I have to hammer the other person senseless, or do I just need to focus on my job of upholding quality?
- Have I felt these intense feelings before in a prior situation?
- Should I seek help to maintain my professionalism?

If you decide you need help, make sure you choose trustworthy people. Here are some sources for you to consider:

- your directors' or other professional support group
- your mentor
- your online professional development network
- your agency's employee relations department
- an otherwise experienced professional whom you respect and who respects you
- a highly recommended counselor or therapist, whom you will interview before hiring as your advisor

Talking through what you may be overlaying on your current dilemma will help both your amygdala and your executive function. Both parts of your brain will also help you. Your amygdala has alerted you that there's potential danger if you take action before you are ready. With help, you can use the amygdala's passion to fuel your desire to do the right thing. Capitalize on the amygdala's energy while using your tools to call out your executive function.

Your prefrontal cortex is resourceful. You'll find you'll be able to come up with alternative solutions, role-play possibilities, and select the best approach to the situation. By the time you have talked everything through and practiced what you might do, you will have taken the first steps down the pathway to resolution, from amygdala to prefrontal cortex.

With these actions in place, your response to the conflict will be appropriate, prepared, and more confident. And if you need help, you will also have a support system in place. Use your tools to calm yourself down if your buttons get pushed during the interaction with the other person.

Yalena's Aha Moment about Overlay

While talking with her directors' support group in confidence, Yalena levels that she wants to fire Trixie Marie without due process (adhering to the program's "three strikes and you're out," progressive discipline policy), even though she knows that is not a smart approach. She shares that Trixie Marie reminds her of that nasty Jessica who betrayed her in high school. Other directors share their stories of similar challenges, histories, and successes. One of them plays the role of Trixie Marie. Yalena laughs and cries her way to a reasonable solution. Before she takes action with Trixie Marie, Yalena makes sure she has documented everything and that her actions are in compliance with program standards. She gets backup from her personnel department, board chair, and/or attorney.

When she confronts Trixie Marie, Yalena has devoted enough time to living in her executive function that she is confident she will be able to bounce back from (or take breaks during) the confrontation as needed. In fact, while meeting with Trixie Marie, Yalena's heart pounds, and her mouth goes dry. However, she takes a breath and—yes!—remembers to picture Trixie Marie in her underwear.

Yalena has given herself a second chance to be the professional she is by using all the tools and understanding at her disposal. Trixie Marie gets the message: shape up or ship out. What do you think Trixie Marie will decide?

Call on the Executive Function or Surrender to the Amygdala: The Choice Is Yours

We all have learned how to survive, or we wouldn't be here today. As educators, however, we want far more than survival. We want to make a difference. We want to give and receive second chances.

Although we can use survival tactics learned in childhood—invisibility, denial, playing dumb, self-effacement, and bullying—as adults, we can all step back to claim more mature choices. We can rise above the patterns to find hope. In fact, with an attitude of gratitude, I can thank my childhood limitations for introducing me to adult possibilities. As the saying goes, "It's never too late to have a happy childhood." Likewise, it's never too late to be happy as an adult. Know this: the happier you become, the happier those around you will be.

We all deserve a soothing life of second chances, uncluttered by all these "tough bully" distractions.

Reflection Questions

1. Like Yalena, have you faced unresolved conflicts that push your buttons? What's the conflict? What behaviors are getting under your skin? What calming techniques work for you? Is overlay getting in the way? If you can look up, what second chance awaits you when you squarely face off against the Bully of Fear?

2. Think of the behaviors that push your buttons and cause you to lose perspective: What did you read in this chapter that would be most helpful in dealing with button pushers? What skills do you have already that work? What new skills or strategies might you be willing to apply to a difficult situation?

3. Overlay is an issue that often requires additional outside professional help. What trusted resources are available to you and your staff/colleagues? How can you find out how these providers and resources are rated by others? What do you do if a colleague/staff member who needs professional help refuses to seek that help?

4. Has anyone in your life served as your Eleanor Roosevelt, the person who mentors or helps you keep perspective? When you recall what this person has said or advised you, what helped you the most? Are you serving as a mentor to others in this way? If so, what have you learned from the process about dealing with the Bully of Fear?

5. Most of us know the story of Beauty and the Beast, just like we may know the Rapunzel or Goldilocks stories. Think of a children's story,

There is a wisdom that is woe; but there is a woe that is madness. And there is a Catskill eagle in some souls that can alike dive down into the blackest gorges, and soar out of them again and become invisible in the sunny spaces.

And even if he forever flies within the gorge, that gorge is in the mountains; so that even in his lowest swoop the mountain eagle is still higher than the other birds upon the plain, even though they soar.
—Herman Melville, Moby Dick

fairy tale, or fable that offers lessons on how to cope effectively with fear, bullies, and/or self-doubt. If you were to write one of these stories, how would you tell the story, and what message would you want readers to hear? Imagine the story Yalena could write, given her experience with her former, supposed best friend, Jessica, and onetime boyfriend, Moses.

Chapter 5

 Acknowledging Attractive Distractions

The Internet seizes our attention, only to scatter it.—*Nicholas Carr*

So Many Distractions

Second chances await us at every moment. However, alluringly attractive distractions can sweep us out of the moment and into buzzing realms of excitement and novelty: Have you ever started a web search that took you on a wild goose chase? In the end, one distraction leads us to another distraction until we wonder, what was the question?

Lovely as our quiet, restorative moments are, like my reflective moment at the lakeside in Vermont in chapter 4, these second-chance invitations can too easily be elbowed out by cotton-candy distractions. Moments of awe, moments of noticing the wonder of where we are—those moments are always available to us. Since that's the case, why do we open ourselves to so few of those moments, especially now that we know the simple process to access such moments?

Sure, threats push our buttons so we can't see straight, but what robs us of second chances during our easier, quieter moments? As much as I want to experience a MIM (meditation in moment), I can just as easily skip the chance. Why?

Let's level with one another about what distracts us so effectively from seeking the beauty of each moment. Let's begin the treasure hunt to find our second chance in any moment.

Daily habits, if unchallenged, can slip into addictive behavior: Tonight, I eat dark chocolate; tomorrow, I need dark chocolate. If an addiction is something we have to lie about, we may be distracting ourselves with a substance like sugar or a process like overworking to avoid the moment. As we self-medicate against discomfort in the moment, we also knock ourselves out of the realm of liberating second chances.

The good news: Powerful second chances call to us at all times, including when we are distracted by old habits, inattention, conflict, rejection, weariness, or discouragement. Remarkably (at first glance), second chances thrive in the places where we least expect them.

Daily Distractions: Running Ragged with Overcommitment

Think of your typical day and the million things chattering away at you: work responsibilities, financial responsibilities, family responsibilities, friend responsibilities, household responsibilities, medical responsibilities, physical fitness responsibilities, healthy nutrition responsibilities, responsibility responsibilities. Feeling overwhelmed by just one of these responsibilities can detonate the amygdala. You know how you feel when multiple demands chatter at you all at the same time. When our shoulders are laden, we automatically look downward from the weight.

Educators are all about commitment. Responsibilities grow out of our commitments. Responsibilities extend our commitments. Responsibilities breed responsibilities. Responsible people are asked to take on more responsibilities.

Ever wonder where the passion went in your life? In our quest to do the right thing, we overwhelm our days and nights with responsibilities. We stress ourselves into worrying:

- Am I making a difference or just running in place?
- Have I sacrificed meaning for security?
- Am I doing all that I am meant to do?
- Am I up-to-date on the latest research?
- Can I pay my bills?

- Am I devoting enough quality time to my family?
- Am I facing or preparing for the realities of getting older?
- Has predictability hit the delete button on awe and wonder?
- What are my everyday choices and actions modeling for children?

Our amygdala eats stress for breakfast, lunch, and dinner, and grazes endlessly during the hours in between. As responsibilities elbow out joy, the amygdala puts in a full day (and night) at work. The eagle that once soared can't find a way out of the confines of its pretty aviary at the zoo.

Your responsibilities, your work, your to-do list, your most pressing task, that difficult conversation you have been avoiding, your text messages, e-mails, calls: each of these awaits you, tapping its foot.

With all of these distractions in play, giving yourself a break might seem impossible. You might miss something important, or, worse, waste a moment, which would mean even more demands pile up on you. The Bully of Fear intimidates us, especially when we are too busy to notice.

Nobody else can live the life you live. And even though no human being is perfect, we always have the chance to bring what's unique about us to live in a redeeming way.
—Fred Rogers

The Pretty Distractions: Seduced by the Internet

These days, we cannot talk about everyday habits, distractions, and living in the moment without acknowledging the Internet's impact. Our relationship with the Internet is intricately related to our ability to seek out and accept second chances. Has your relationship to the screen given you freedom, enslavement, or both?

I know how compelling and useful the Internet is. At the same time, I believe many of us educators would admit that the Internet can be an alluring distraction. Think, for example, of how you react when you hear the ping of a new e-mail appearing in your inbox. Do you feel compelled to check it right away, just in case it's about something important that needs to be tended to immediately? Or do you limit your text messaging and e-mailing to predetermined and finite times a day to limit distractions? Being at the mercy of your inbox—or the latest news, stock reports, texts from a friend, or updates on social media, for that matter—can rob you of the ability to look up and notice what's going on around you. You need to find ways to open yourself to second chances during those times when your attention is riveted to the screen.

Comfort in Little Things

Give yourself permission to turn off or away from your screens at least one hour before you go to bed. What soothes you and helps you become drowsy? Do you have a book you have been wanting to read or music you would like to hear? Or how about spending warm cuddling time with your special person or pet?

Technology like the Internet is a marvel in itself: a grandparent thousands of miles away can Skype with his granddaughter; classrooms of children in Mozambique can talk and laugh with children in America; we can access limitless information with the mere click of a few keys; autistic children can discover the world; Stephen Hawking can write his books and speak aloud.

At the same time, screen time can usurp our face-to-face time, the relational time that is crucial for young children's learning. Remember what happened to the children while teacher Lyra was texting? In the moments we remove ourselves from human connection, we send the message to the people around us that they rate a distant second on our list of priorities.

Not convinced that the Internet not just focuses, but also scatters, your attention? Consider these statistics documented by Daniel Levitin (2014) in his recent article "Hit the Reset Button in Your Brain." He cites a 2011 study revealing that:

- on an average day people are exposed to five times the amount of information that they were exposed to in 1986;
- people watch an average of five hours of TV each day, from the eighty-five thousand hours of programming produced per day; and
- for every YouTube video watched, another 5,999 hours of new video are posted.

Caught in the Web of Information

Anyone caught up in the news stream on political battles, sports, reality stars, human dramas, epidemics, and natural disasters knows how all-consuming that information can be. With the advent of smartphones, we can check the latest crisis in the news as easily as we can check stocks, weather, sports scores, blood pressure, or calories consumed, twenty-four hours a day, seven days a week, no matter where we might be in the world. This easy access to ever-more information adds to our stress level and can interfere with our ability to notice second chances. The more we use the Internet, the more we "can't live without" the Internet.

Choosing When to Disconnect

Do you know anyone who might be addicted to the Internet or to her iPhone? Larry Rosen warns that we easily and unconsciously become addicted to accessing the latest data on everything. "Phantom vibration syndrome" is evidence of that addiction, according to Rosen (2012). Have you ever gone on alert (thanks to your amygdala), believing that your iPhone is vibrating, only to find you imagined that? Thirty-five percent of us check our text and e-mail messages before we do anything else in the morning (54). Our iPhones have become our oxygen tanks.

Can we find a balance? Can we allow soulful spaces to lift us out of our Internet hypervigilance? Let me offer you an alternative way of thinking about the Internet. Most of us think that if we want to be professionals, we have no choice but to pay attention, stay informed, work hard, buckle down, suit up, and keep up with the latest research. But how else might we relate to the Internet? In fact, can we notice what truly matters in that stream of information with our nose-to-the-grindstone ways? Or will the Internet (and/or our impossible standards for ourselves to be and do it all) flatline our ability to prioritize?

Rosen offers practical tips on how to change our relationship with the Internet from one of distraction or compulsion to one of second chances. Here's one example: How do you feel at staff meetings when everyone's attention is on their thumbs? They are texting, checking messages, and surfing the Internet while the director or a colleague is trying to engage everyone in fruitful problem solving. Their attention to the business of education has been scattered to the allure of more new information.

Rosen suggests the following practice to engage staff in the moment, where they are more likely to be creative and more likely to discover second chances and innovative ways to resolve problems:

- Ask everyone to turn off her iPhone and place it face down on the table.

- Advise everyone not to worry; you will take an iPhone break every fifteen minutes, so they will not be disconnected for any longer than that.

- Appoint a staff member to signal when each fifteen-minute period ends.

- Select the staff member who is most uncomfortable being disconnected to take on this task.

- Watch what happens!

Give Yourself a Break

Choose a nickname for the technology you depend on most (e.g., texting, Facebook, Internet surfing). Tell your Jorge or Myrtle one limitation you are placing on your time together. Use that time to connect with someone or something you love.

In my experience, everyone gets so engaged in face-to-face small-group discussions or in large-group debate and problem-solving activities that they forget about their iPhones! In fact, the staff member appointed to keep time is often the most astonished by how engaging people can be.

Help with Distractions, from Neuroscientists

To listen to my two interviews with Rosen, go to www .bamradionetwork .com and type "Larry Rosen" into the search box.

Recent and forever-burgeoning studies on the adult brain offer liberating avenues into worlds we only hoped were there. Those patterns we thought we were locked into are just that: patterns. Patterns can be changed. When we enter that zone of questioning patterns, a world of possibilities flocks to us like geese to warmer weather.

Much like Rosen, Levitin challenges our assumptions about paying attention. He says we can accomplish more if we understand recent research. Our evolving brain, Levitin clarifies, has two modes of attention.

Task-positive mode is that focused, intentional, nose-to-the-grindstone way of paying attention. We use task-positive mode to work our way through our checklists and to tackle tough assignments. Task-positive adults are applauded.

Task-negative attention comes to life when we daydream, let our attention wander, look up at the sky, or notice a child's shy smile. Task-negative mode frees our spirit. Task-negative adults are seen as spacey or, worse, lazy. According to Levitin, our brain constantly shifts between the two modes—hypervigilant nose to the grindstone and whimsy. The insula, located approximately one inch beneath the skull from the crown of the head, is that fulcrum part of our brain that tips the balance from hypervigilance to daydreaming.

Sure, we have to focus or be "task positive," but we also need to allow for those fleeting moments of insight that pass like fireflies in the summer twilight. Creativity blooms if we devote finite time to the infinite. In short, we need to daydream and pay attention to our musings.

Levitin suggests we structure our day in order to devote finite time to the task positives:

- reading and responding to text messages and e-mails
- making phone calls
- working on projects

He also urges us to claim time for the task negatives, or pure moments of daydreaming by:

- stepping outside,
- observing something of beauty, or
- playing and laughing.

As Levitin explains, "Daydreaming leads to creativity, and creative activities teach us agency, the ability to change the world, to mold it to our liking, to have a positive effect on our environment" (Levitin 2014). Who wouldn't want the gift of "agency," that power to make a difference?

Changing the world for the better is our job as educators. I know you want to leave the world a better place for the children in your life. So let's begin the process of claiming second chances. Let's take one step at a time into the world of wonderment. A simple process can lift you up and out of the mundane to wonderment. Remember, each moment we live in wonder pays off twofold as we return to the task-positive world.

As you read Miranda's case study below, pay attention to what part of your brain clicks in: your problem-solving task-positive nature, your free-floating imagination that envisions totally new approaches, or both. Notice also the distractions, the habits, or even the addictions that interfere with Miranda's intention to be a productive director.

CASE STUDY   *Miranda the Workaholic, Web-Surfing Director*

Early childhood director Miranda has trouble saying no. She wants everyone on her staff to be happy and content. She is willing to work eighteen-hour days if that's what it takes to keep her program the most up-to-date and desirable in town. Miranda scans the Internet whenever she gets a free moment to read the latest research on new classroom practices that benefit young children.

Because parents know Miranda believes in being accessible, they text her anytime, night or day. Teachers know Miranda will cover for them if they need to take a day or two of personal time, even if they let her know at the last minute. At home, Miranda expects herself to be the most competent mom and partner she can be.

Her assistant, Maurice, is frustrated that Miranda rarely gives him any "real" tasks; he feels Miranda has trouble delegating and trusting him with anything important. She pays more attention to the screen than she does to Maurice.

Maurice decides he is no longer willing to be Miranda's assistant unless she delegates more substantive responsibilities to him. He could easily read and evaluate all that research and provide Miranda with the most relevant studies. In fact, Maurice believes that if she would notice him, Miranda would discover he has some innovative research-based practices to recommend.

Maurice asks Miranda to meet with him at a café nearby after work. In his straightforward way, Maurice says: "Miranda, if you don't take care of yourself, you won't be around to take care of anyone else. What will it take for you to see that you need to delegate, set boundaries on your time with staff and on the Internet, and just lighten up? We all love you, but we are worried about you. How can I help? Honestly, if you don't let me do more, I cannot be your assistant. I feel like you don't trust me to take any of the load off your shoulders."

Everyone has been made for some particular work, and the desire for that work has been put in every heart.—Rumi

---

What second chance awaits Miranda in this moment? What would it take for Miranda to change? What would Miranda need to let go? Have you been in Miranda's situation? What helps you look up to see options you otherwise would never have seen?

Learning from Children and the Child within Us: Letting Go of an Entrenched Habit When It Feels Impossible

Consider an experience involving habit I had as a child, detailed below, as you reflect on what might help Miranda. Habits inhabit us! They take over and determine our actions. Changing entrenched habits can be daunting.

How often have you made a New Year's resolution with the best of intentions? You were ready to change a pattern of behavior that wasn't good for you, such as not working out, not eating healthfully, or not delegating. But before long, daily life, with its compelling task-positive demands, intervened. You had meetings that couldn't be rescheduled, you had to deal with crises that popped up, or you just couldn't summon the energy needed to "live up to" your resolution. How human is that? The majority of us who make resolutions find ourselves unable to carry out the practices we know would make our lives better.

My hunch is that you have also made a commitment or a resolution that you have honored. Sticking to that resolution changed your life for the better. Anyone who gives up smoking will attest to this.

Can we be task negative in situations? Can a resolution to change a pattern be an open door rather than another loathsome task on our to-do list?

Here's how I came up with a task-negative resolution I followed, and it changed my life for the better. Perhaps my child self could teach my adult self something about having the courage to make a positive change.

Today most people would call me an extrovert; I love interacting with large groups of people, engaging in spirited conversations with strangers as well as friends, and meeting new friends as I fly around the country and the world for my work as an educator. As a child, I was the opposite. As a first grader, I was younger than my classmates, and I felt bashful and awkward; I was not good at making friends.

So I made a resolution: I would walk into second grade acting as if I were outgoing and at ease with anyone. I smiled and walked through the door of Mrs. DeSilva's class, crossing my fingers that second grade would be more welcoming than first grade had been. I reminded myself to stride into my second-grade class every day as if I were worry-free and confident.

Guess what? My resolution worked. Because of my friendly ways, I was chosen early for teams and I could speak up when a teacher called on me. I rarely went back on my resolution. I didn't like being left out. I trusted my imagination to envision a better way, and the result of that trust was a happier childhood. I let go of a pattern, one crossed-fingers day at a time, without knowing what I was doing. I just wanted to be happier. My task-negative self told me I could be happier.

I didn't realize it then, but now I see that I gave myself a second chance. At home I was to "be seen and not heard." At school I could talk and sing and play. Although I had never heard the phrase then, I was "faking it 'til I (could) make it," and it worked.

Watch children as they invent new ways. Watch the imaginative, playful child in yourself envision a different and freer way of being. In any moment, we can give ourselves a second chance. In that moment, we can find inspiration that just might change everything that follows.

Sometimes all it takes is acknowledging that being task negative (our playful, daydreaming self) is every bit as valuable as being task positive (working and working and working). Let's see how learning of this practice from a child might help Miranda.

Miranda's Evolution from Frantic Task Positive to More-Relaxed Task Negative

As Miranda listens to her assistant, Maurice, she is first stunned: "I thought I was doing what everyone needs me to do: staying on top of the latest research, looking out for staff, connecting with families, making myself available. Come to think of it, I am in a frenzy. But I don't know how to let up."

Maurice reminds her: "Look, you have developed your team admirably. We all respect you, but we worry about you. Let me do some of the research, for example, and keep you posted on what's relevant to us. If I do the research, I could also do a weekly update for teachers that includes reflection questions. That would make it easier for us to discuss the latest practices at our staff meeting. Imagine what you could do with the extra time you would have freed up."

Miranda agrees to think about what Maurice has said and get back to him. She lets him know she appreciates his willingness to level with her; she comes close to apologizing for undervaluing him.

When she gets home that night, Miranda notices her children and partner are all on their iPhones or tablets. They barely say "hi" when she walks in the door. Instead of checking her own messages, Miranda takes time to play (!) with their yellow lab, Tica. Miranda's daughter, Rosie, notices and joins her. Miranda and Rosie actually talk with each other about their day. Miranda imagines, "What if I did this every day? It's just five minutes."

At school the next day, Miranda asks Maurice to monitor the Internet; she will go to the infant room to rock a baby. Maybe even sing a lullaby. Maybe even take in the fresh baby smell and touch the softness of the baby's hair. Maybe even remember what she loved about singing to her own children.

The Internet as Bully?

The Internet is a liberator. Technology saves lives. Children learn rapidly with their fingertips. Classrooms can be enhanced by incorporating technology and plugging into children's already "plugged-in" lives.

Addictions are not limited to substances (like vodka or sugar). As Rosen warns, processes like work and Internet usage can also tip into addictions. I know this well: I am a recovering work addict.

Addictive behavior is compulsive behavior. When we are addicted, we stop making a choice; we act compulsively. We have to check our latest messages online. We have to consume a piece of chocolate. We have to finish everything on our to-do list. We have to do these things right now!

We can allow the Internet to bully us into subservience, or we can step back, go on a "digital diet," detox, and begin again to discover the joys of interconnection. Just as staff members can come to life interactively when their cell phones are off-limits, so too can Miranda reclaim joy in singing a lullaby to a baby. The Internet itself is not a bad thing; our compulsion to overuse the Internet, that's the bad thing.

Give yourself and the people around you a second chance to discover the moment. Consider Rosen's advice. Tune into either of my two interviews with Rosen at BAMradionetwork.com Leadership Strategies. Rosen offers strategies to restore balance through forming a healthy relationship with the Internet.

Second Chances Waiting for Me in the University Library

A few years ago when I returned to my undergraduate school to give a presentation, I decided to stop by the library for some last-minute research. Back in my day, the Douglass College (of Rutgers University) library was lined with book stacks, which I adored. Because most of those stacks had been replaced with computers, I pulled out a chair and bellied up to the Internet. As I searched for recent studies on attention and the brain, I let my mind wander a bit. I looked out the window onto the campus, I noticed the librarians helping students, I breathed in the air, and I recalled the wonder of being an undergraduate discovering her world. I loved those early Saturday mornings in the "libe." I loved discovering how other people understood the world. I loved reading, and I loved the quiet.

In that moment of gratitude, I fell in love once again with learning every moment and with how I could change and grow thanks to seeing my world anew. *Kaboom*: a second chance awaited me as I allowed the wonder of the moment to take me deeper to a place of awe.

Research is how we live: we find out something new to live our lives more fully. Old habits, like using books instead of the web, or iPhones instead of face-to-face conversation, can stick to us like lichens on a rock. However, in the very choice to notice where we are, even when under the sway of a habit, we can free ourselves. I looked up from the Internet and saw a seventeen-year-old me in a state of wonder that the world was far wider than I had ever imagined in my tiny hometown in upstate New York.

In the comfort of little things, like opening to a long-forgotten memory, we find our second chance. We need only step away enough from what has a hold on us to see what awaits us.

Reflection Questions

1. Have you ever found yourself in a frenzy like Miranda did, but had no idea how to stop? What in Miranda's story reminds you of yourself? What is one step you could take, even if for only five minutes a day, to step out of the frenzy and breathe? Do you have a favorite pet who would love your attention? What if you said to someone you love, "Let's just hang out together for a while?"

2. Take a moment: Recall a commitment or resolution to change for the better that you made and carried out. How did that choice change your life? Where did you find support? What inner strength did you call on? If at times you went back to old patterns, were you able to forgive yourself and begin again?

3. When has a child helped you see the world anew? What was your state of mind/heart before you fully engaged with the child? What happened in the presence of the child that opened your eyes? When you reflect on that moment, what changed in you and your attitude?

4. How have New Year's resolutions served you (or not worked for you)? What makes the difference between a commitment we follow through on and one that we allow to fall by the wayside? Are New Year's resolutions worthwhile anymore?

5. Has compulsive behavior—checking online messages, working twelve-hour days, eating what's in front of you rather than what's healthy for you—ever driven you? If so, what helps or might help you step back, detox, and reclaim a more balanced life where second chances abound?

Chapter 6

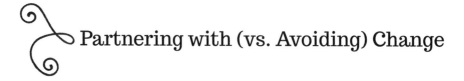

Partnering with (vs. Avoiding) Change

You were born with wings. You are not meant for crawling, so don't.
You have wings. Learn to use them and fly.—*Rumi*

To most folk, change is neither a pretty thought nor a sought-after dynamic.
When one school was looking for a new leader, the faculty settled on the
inside candidate despite his lack of leadership experience outside of the
classroom. "The devil you know is better than the devil you don't know," is
the adage upon which they based their "safe" decision.

   Wouldn't it be great if the children were always safe from harm? We
parents (and educators) do all we can to protect children from getting hurt.
The core value of our professional organization, the National Association for
the Education of Young Children (NAEYC), is "do no harm."

   Here's the challenge: If we don't change, we stagnate. If we stagnate,
we can no longer model life skills for children. Adam Bryant's research on
leadership reveals that "passionate curiosity," "battle-hardened confidence,"
and "team smarts" are the traits of successful leaders (2011, 12). In short,
successful leaders change.

   Change involves loss of something to gain something else. Loss evokes
sadness, anger, and weariness, none of which is the easiest emotion to feel.
So, it's no surprise that a major stumbling block on the pathway to second
chances is fear of change. Fear is a cranky thing. Few of us like to feel

fearful, sad, lonely, angry, or weary. As we struggle to avoid these unwelcome feelings, we are in danger of eliminating second chances. After all, any second chance involves leaving behind the first chance. Any second chance is a change. Where we stand on the continuum from fearing change to accepting change can indicate how open we are to taking and giving second chances.

Turns out our adult brain hve their own take on second chances. As we have noted, our neurons are set up to fight against, run from, or run with second chances. Thanks to the aforementioned brain research, we know more than ever about what "gets under our skin," "pushes our buttons," and helps us "keep our eyes on the prize." If we pay attention to what's going on inside of us, we can, with practice, learn to identify stress indicators and ultimately free ourselves for the joy of giving and taking second chances. We can partner with, rather than resist, change.

Waiting for Woolly Caterpillar's Prophecy

He's prickly, fuzzy, chunky, and stubbly. He's coal black with a wide, burnt-orange belly band. He knows where he is going. His velvety body undulates in a deliberate and clunky wave over fallen leaves. When I place him gently in the palm of my hand, he wads into a "Put me down! I'm busy!" ball.

Small, backbone-free, and vulnerable, my woolly caterpillar is wise. He predicts the length and severity of our northern winters. When his orange belly-band is wide, severe winters follow. If black prevails, winter will be as gentle and short as my fuzzy friend.

Woolly caterpillar and his siblings telegraph their forecast each year to anyone close enough to the earth to listen: short-long-short or long-short-long. As a child, I trusted my woolly friends. As an adult, I trust them still.

When orange dominated last fall, I moved quickly to plant 422 spring-blooming bulbs. When snow weighed down the earth more and more heavily, and ice pressed down the snow, winter-weary folk complained. I thanked Woolly C.

In New England, we call long-lasting snow "poor man's fertilizer." My daffodils, tulips, and crocuses were well protected and nourished throughout their four-month hibernation.

On these mid-April days, I walk from garden to garden, scanning for the green breaking through coffee-brown soil. Finding more and more sprouted bulbs each day, I bow to the Woolly C. His tiny presence reminds me to trust that on the coldest, darkest days, flower bulbs quietly gather energy.

No matter how harsh and long and dreary the winter, bulbs burst into pink, yellow, and lavender blossoms every spring. No matter how painful and dispiriting the conflicts of life, second chances are guaranteed. This morning bouquets burst before my eyes, where not long ago, dirty snow pressed heavily on the ground.

I am grateful for a childhood out-of-doors with wondrous friends like woolly caterpillars, fireflies, "peepers," dragonflies, and Monarch butterflies. Each of these tiny, vulnerable beings offers the message that beauty prevails and second chances return in every season of life.

—Holly Elissa, April 30, 2014

Internal Resistance to and Passion for Second Chances

Why would anyone say no to a second chance, especially if taking that chance could lead to liberation, serenity, and joy?

Try this . . .

Find a pen and a piece of paper. Place the pen in your hand, and prepare to write your full name on the paper in that cursive, curling, rolling script we learned in elementary school but that many children are no longer required to learn. Prepare to write your full name (middle name, original surname if you changed your name—whatever you and your culture have established as your name). Ready?

Okay, stop. Place your pen in your opposite hand (your nondominant hand), and begin writing now.

Your pain is the breaking of the shell that encloses your understanding.
—Khalil Gibran

How does writing with your opposite hand feel? Uncomfortable? Awkward? Slow? Messy? Out of control? Fun? Challenging? Like you are five years old or perhaps ninety years old? How does your writing look to you? Acceptable? Embarrassing? Fascinating? Surprisingly legible?

In those few seconds of writing with your opposite hand, you stressed and challenged your brain. In fact, in a small way, you threatened your brain. You also gave your brain an opportunity to forge new neural pathways. As we have discussed, one part of our brains, the amygdala, appears to eschew change. Another part of our brains, our prefrontal cortex, readily adapts to the challenge.

Whichever part of the brain "clicks in" determines what we do next. We either resist change, or we dive into the stream. Our brains are wired to keep us safe from threat and in harmony with our surroundings and peers. Our brains are also wired to help us grow, be inspired, and remain optimistic. So much depends on which part of our brains are activated when we are given a second chance. As we will also see, so much depends on the choices we make when we feel the discomfort or the jolt of change.

If I'm keeping my head down to survive the day, I am not free to notice a second chance, even if it bounces up and down, waving to capture my attention. We need food in our bellies and a solid roof over our heads before we can climb out of survival mode and begin to walk our spiritual pathway. Consider Abraham Maslow's hierarchy of needs, which progresses up the scale from survival to spirituality.

All the evidence that we have indicates that it is reasonable to assume in practically every human being, and certainly in almost every newborn baby, that there is an active will toward health, an impulse toward growth, or toward the actualization.
—Abraham Maslow

John Medina nails this principle as well: we need to feel safe enough from threats and fear of threats to look up and notice the possibilities all around us (Medina, Sporleder, DeWitt, and Stewart, "Creating Safe Learning Spaces for Traumatized Children").

Sanctuaries for Growing and Changing

No wonder we work so hard to help children feel safe at school, a sanctuary where each child's nutritional and physical well-being needs are met. Just feeling safe enough to nap is life changing for some children. In a secure and loving environment, children can begin to learn the social-emotional skills they need to negotiate their world. A wary child who allows you to hold her on your lap has found a sanctuary in your presence. When a child's spirit is progressively uncramped, she can unfold to become who she is meant to be.

An amaryllis bulb, long forgotten in the dark cellar of winter, will unfurl itself to flourish when bathed in light, tucked into rich soil, nourished with water, and tended regularly. Green shoots become leaves, and a tight bud opens into a powerful pop of color that lasts and lasts. Wounded spirits have far more difficulty making it out of the cellar. Even positive change can look like a threat at first.

Sanctuaries for Learning

As a preschool teacher over the many years, [I] have seen so many children from the urban community of Boston gone through so many extremes; hearing gunshots, the ringing alarm of ambulance, fire trucks, police emergencies. These alarms can be themselves or family members from their home. . . . these parents and children are coming from these disorganized homes. They still find trust, joy, and comfort in the classrooms/teachers. It is a pleasure to see them coming in the doors of our preschool smiling, telling their sad and good stories, looking forward to our healthy food, safe classrooms, playing with others like themselves, and discussing making it through life. Today my pleasure is seeing and hearing about a student that came out doing right in the community. "Oh, how I love teaching . . . that is so right!"
—Shawna Brown, May 21, 2014

The positive change of healing, although initially resisted, has the power to win over even the fearful parts of ourselves.

*What Difference Would It Make If You Gave Someone,
Including Yourself, a Second Chance? Shelby the Rescue Dog
Rescues Back*

Right now, in a school in rural South Carolina, North Carolina, or Georgia, a dog once abandoned, beaten, or neglected is using her second chance to rescue a hurting child. Picture Shelby prancing beside her trainer through the front door of a school and, in a heartbeat, intuitively selecting a child.

The child Shelby selects may act as if she is "just fine," or he may be a cocky bully or a child emotionally isolated from others. Just as Shelby was hurled to the side of the road, the child she chooses—regardless of appearance—has in some way been abandoned, beaten, or neglected. Shelby senses a fellow traveler.

Shelby will figure out just the right way to connect with the child: Does resting her furry brown head on the child's lap thaw the child's icy shield? Do Shelby's imploring amber eyes see through the child's defenses to his wounded heart? Or does Shelby's 100 percent wagging body, offering the child 100 percent unconditional love, forge the connection?

Adele Little, educator and dog expert, describes this moment as Shelby "loving on" the child until the child cannot hold back from petting the adoring dog. In that moment, the dog with the second chance soothes the wounded spirit of the child who needs a second chance. In that moment of wonder, a healing connection is forged.

I believe your experience with a second chance could uplift the rest of us.

Can you share a time when you, like Shelby, gave another person or yourself a second chance?

Do you know a child who needs Shelby?

Can you picture the easing of the child's tense exterior when Shelby selects the child?

Can you also picture Shelby ambling your way?

How would your soul be eased if you gave yourself a second chance?

Fred Rogers could answer these questions. He reminds us: "The toughest thing to do is to forgive the person who has hurt you, especially if that person is yourself" (Rogers 2005).

—Holly Elissa, March 26, 2014

The Eye of the Storm: Addressing Change in the Moment

Here's an example of how the amygdala deals with any change, any new event. Toddler teacher Annie Mae is reading to a small group of contented children when she senses that Gabrielo is bored. When Gabrielo is bored, he gets frustrated. When Gabrielo gets frustrated enough, he bites. Sacha, beside Gabrielo, is enrapt with every word and image of the book. Gabrielo's quick turn toward Sacha sets off Annie Mae's alarms. In a heartbeat, Annie Mae intervenes, swooping to pick up Gabrielo and separate him from Sacha, while motioning for her aide, Aleta, to continue reading.

Seeing a child threatened or about to melt down, Annie Mae's heart rate increases. An adrenaline blast strengthens her muscles for quick action. That surge of adrenaline gives us more strength and quickness than we ever thought we had. A petite mother catches a dresser before it falls forward onto her baby. An athlete leaps farther than she ever has before. Grandpa, who has arthritis, runs to the bus to prevent excited grandchildren from spilling onto the busy street.

All of this extraordinary power is brought to us by the amygdala gland. Continuously conducting sweeps of our surroundings for threats, the amygdala clicks into action before we can stop to think. Annie Mae sweeps Gabrielo into her arms. Mom saves her baby from a crashing dresser. Grandpa shepherds the children out of harm's way. Who would not be grateful for the amygdala's capacity to serve as our tireless lifeguard?

Annie Mae might not be grateful if that adrenaline surge pushes her to lose her temper. Mom might not be happy if her baby is terrified by Mom's spiking fear. Gramps might not be grateful if he pulls a muscle and can't play with his long-awaited grandchildren.

That storm is going to bring change whether we resist it or not. How can we open ourselves to the second chances that change sweeps to us?

Witnessing Rather Than Getting Dowsed by the Storm: Keeping Perspective during the Change Process

When threatened, we lose perspective. Our cornucopia of choices collapses into one option: survival. The people around us flip into enemies or allies. Red alert splashes all the other colors into darkness. We react. We do not plan or imagine or envision.

Wouldn't it be great if we could lift ourselves up out of the basement of knee-jerk resistance to the balcony of healing perspective? Do you think that's possible? Or do you believe we are always susceptible to being controlled by our fears? This three-step process can help us rise above fear:

1. acknowledge when a threat is hovering,
2. identify what we need to stay sane in the moment, and take action to
3. step out of the tornado's path into a zone of second chances.

This three-step practice lifts us from

- immaturity to maturity,
- self-pity to professionalism, and
- restriction to freedom.

Thanks to the same trigger that once threatened to destroy us, we can free ourselves to see, take, and offer second chances.

In other words, we need to lovingly attend to our spirits. We can learn to free ourselves from the control of knee-jerk reactions. We do this by first paying attention to our bodies' alert systems. Give yourself permission to acknowledge—not just to react to—the indicators that your amygdala is overtaking you. Stepping back like this for perspective reopens the door to the wonder of second chances.

Consider these two slogans, used by people in twelve-step recovery. Each slogan provides practical, no-nonsense tips on how to keep our eyes on the prize when our resistance overtakes our hope for change.

HALT, a twelve-step acronym for

- **H**ungry,
- **A**ngry,
- **L**onely, or
- **T**ired,

reminds us to halt before making important decisions when we are on edge.

Another acronym, WAIT, encourages us to wait before we open our mouths to say something we might regret:

- **W**hy
- **A**m
- **I**
- **T**alking?

By HALTing and WAITing for resistance to pass, we can breathe or pray our way into being more conscious about the benefits of change.

Reading the Signs of Change

The physical indicators that your amygdala gland is taking control of the change process are predictable. That very predictability frees us to regain perspective. You know the amygdala is spiking when you:

- feel suddenly "on alert;"
- don't feel as safe as you felt a minute before;
- sense a change in your heartbeat or a clenching around your heart;
- breathe more quickly and perhaps more shallowly;
- virtually feel the hair stand up on the back of your neck (imagine a dog's "rough");
- notice your leg muscles tensing (preparing to crouch for a fight or tighten for a run);
- note your eyes are scanning your environment; and
- feel a compulsion to react (feel the need to get out of there, to smack the "offender," or to rip away the surface chitchat and "get to the bottom" of the problem).

Awareness of this dynamic affords us the freedom to take a step back, use tools to calm our heart, and regain perspective. Awareness and acceptance of this process empowers us to take action. We become freer to see the potential gift in the challenge. We allow ourselves to choose second chances more readily. We are more conscious about making a choice to partner with, rather than resist, change. Being gentle with ourselves eases our way.

Even the most serene among us are susceptible to the fears that accompany change. Thich Nhat Hanh, a Vietnamese Buddhist monk nominated for the Nobel Peace Prize, stands as a model of serenity in the midst of warfare and injustice. His writings encourage gentleness and loving kindness in the midst of change. Yet, even Thich Nhat Hanh admits fear has overtaken him. After one of his presentations, an assistant found the monk bent over outside the lecture hall, trembling. Nhat Hanh admitted that a belligerent person in the audience had brought back old fears. Overlay had destroyed the moment's grace.

Being fearful is as human as joy. We are complex beings. The reflective and peaceful words of Nhat Hanh are sprinkled throughout this book. Knowing the man devoted to peace is himself human and susceptible to fear reminds us to be gentle with ourselves. The change process, however, does grow easier as we come to see the possibility change offers for a happier world.

Fear of change is as natural as breathing. However, opening our hearts to second chances can also become natural. Now that we have identified the power of fear, let's step up to identifying the power of hope. Understanding that change promises something better helps make facing our discomforts and defenses possible. When we resist change, we are likely to experience:

* denial (pretending the status quo isn't being challenged);
* isolation (keeping our fears to ourselves and not sharing our concern);
* guilt (beating ourselves up for not being more flexible); and
* despair (feeling overtaken by fear).

Each one of these stages of resistance embodies its own antidote for healing:

* Acknowledging that change is in the air eliminates denial.
* Talking with others about our fears (and hopes) overcomes the tendency to isolate ourselves.
* Accepting responsibility to do what we can to change and/or to admit our resistance relieves us of guilt's control.
* Asking for the help of others while letting go of believing we can control others transforms despair into hopeful action (Bruno 2012).

Give Yourself a Break

Recall one difficult decision you made and acted upon that other people warned you against. How has making that change made your life better, truer to you? Give yourself credit for being able to listen to and act courageously on your inner voice.

I went to the woods because I wished to live deliberately, to front only the essential facts of life, and see if I could not learn what it had to teach, and not, when I came to die, discover that I had not lived.
—Henry David Thoreau

The Comfort in Little Things

When we lose our courage and don't believe we can change, we have a lifeline: Friends can remind us of our gifts and strengths. Friends can remind us of other times we have made changes and felt so much better. Friends can love us through our fears. Friends can also use "tough love" and challenge us to rise above our fear. Call a friend; ask for help. Allow your heart to be comforted.

So many times I have heard, "I've been teaching this way for twenty years, I don't need to change." What does that resistance to growing model for children? Use the strategies in this chapter to help you partner with, rather than war against change. You'll discover a second chance at every stage of the change process.

Reflection Questions

1. Recall a time when you were in the presence of a person who vehemently opposed change. What happened? Was that a learning experience for you or the person in any way? Now recall a time when you dug in your heels to avoid changing. Looking back at your own resistance, what might you have done differently? How did your resistance, and the resistance of the other person, affect the change process and the organization?

2. Consider a change you have made that made your whole life better. At what point did you feel you desired the change to happen more than you were afraid of it happening? What tips would you give a young (or seasoned) teacher on welcoming or avoiding change?

3. Technology continuously changes. Do you resist or partner with technological updates? Are you able to keep up with those changes? How do you feel if you fall behind your peers on expertise with technology? What resources (both external and internal) can help you continuously update your skills?

4. Bottoming out (despair) is a pivotal element in the change process: when we realize we can't deny or resist change any longer, we become open to second chances. What do you say to yourself at times like this, when the change you have resisted is going to happen regardless of your resistance?

5. What can children teach us about responding to change? Give some examples about children's willingness to adapt and change. What is the relationship of wonder and curiosity to change?

Part III   Staking Claim to Our Birthright for Joy

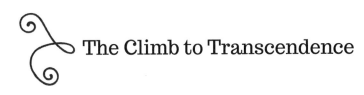

Chapter 7

The Climb to Transcendence

The effort of the genuine spiritual seeker should be to cultivate love until the mind becomes saturated by it.—Bhante Y. Wimala

Living in the moment opens us up to unseen and likely-to-be-missed opportunities. Spirituality follows. As we climb to the spiritual balcony, we see our world differently. A lifetime of second chances on the horizon?

The Amas

Women in tiny, timeless fishing villages along the rough, roiling coastline of Japan practice a unique profession, which they pass on to their daughters. This profession is both rigorously high risk and not the domain of men. The profession is pearl fishing. Pearl fishers are called amas, mermaids of the sea.

Without oxygen tanks or wet suits, pearl fishing women stalwartly hold their breath as they dive beneath the beating waves, carrying a thick knife and a sack for the treasure. They must hold their breath for at least two minutes and not panic. They must be clear of vision and resolute in their purpose. They must focus, remaining calm while under threat. They must find the treasure while not getting greedy. They must hold both themselves and the sea in respect.

Fishers of pearls are steady, stalwart, and determined women. Their livelihoods and indeed their lives depend upon their ability to know exactly where the oysters are likely to harbor pearls. Once they find the oysters, the pearl fishers must work with alacrity to free each treasure and place it securely in their sacks, holding just enough oxygen in their about-to-explode lungs to kick up and up until they at last break the water's surface.

In some ways the women are as crusty as the oysters they seek. The raggedy, gray oyster resists the aggravatingly scratching grain of sand that weasels into its shell. Imagine having such a "thorn in your side." The grain of sand must be akin to our having a hangnail or a cold sore or a stubbed toe: uncomfortable, unwanted, offensive, foreign.

Yet, by coexisting with its irksome roommate, the oyster produces art. Beauty. A luminous pearl. What was initially loathsome becomes a thing of loveliness. By braving an unwelcoming, choppy, and dark journey beneath the surface, pearl fishers also discover a thing of beauty.

A number of spiritual principles are at work here.

Something magical and transformative happens for the resistant oyster and for the frozen women: they wrestle their struggles into gifts, into art, into a thing of transcendence. A magnificent second chance—to rediscover or uncover beauty—is born when we embrace what we fear or loathe or both. When the amas break the water's surface and breathe once again, they emit a unique sound called "sea whistling." This is a primal, one-of-a-kind keening sound. Sea-whistling amas can endure for years; many amas are in their nineties.

Few daughters want to learn the pearl-fishing trade these days. The allure of the city calls them away from their matriarchal destiny.

We are now diving deeper to the crucible from which second chances are born. We have examined the daily portals to second chances:

* Noticing where we are in each moment
* Not letting our buttons get pushed
* Facing fear that threatens to overtake our courage
* Acknowledging and facing our natural resistance to change

Unbidden trials in the form of offensive, repugnant experiences can also nudge us into transformation. Our job is to step up, trust, and act on our belief that pearls will form in the least pleasant of places.

Georges Bizet, the French composer of *Carmen*, was so transported by the courage of these amas who dive for pearls that he wrote an opera for them, simply called *The Pearl Fishers*. Even if you find opera laborious, highfalutin, or otherwise off-putting, you are likely to find the "Pearl Fishers Duet" accessible, lyrical, and full of melodious grace. I love that duet no matter how often I hear it; listening to it is always a chance for reverence in the moment.

Better than words, perhaps, that duet will transport you to the next level of second chances: those we come by when we face the things we do not want to face.

Search for "Pearl Fishers Duet" online, and listen to hear the courage and sorrow and promise of the pearl fishers. Andrea Bocelli and Placido Domingo, for example, have recorded a heavenly version of Bizet's tribute to these brave women.

What Do We Model for Children about How to Deal with Adversity?

When children observe us struggling, what do those children learn about diving deep for a second chance? What did you learn as a child by watching the adults in your life?

As children, we learn how to deal with adversity by paying attention to what adults do and say when they face adversity. Some of the practices adults model and/or teach children are constructive and conducive to giving and receiving second chances. Other practices keep us "stuck" and unable to see possibilities.

The diamond cannot be polished without friction, nor man perfected without trials.—Proverb

Let's look at the practices we model for children in the hope that we can choose to live and model more liberating practices. In liberation, second chances abound. Choosing to climb the pathway to transcendence benefits the children in our lives as well as ourselves. Let's search together for the pathways that lead us to transcend the literal and the known, and deliver us to the wonder of the unknown. Like the amas, we each can dive deeper or climb higher to see what we need to see.

The Amas Offer Us These Spiritual Principles

- Become clear in your purpose.
- Remain resolute against the odds.
- Trust yourself, especially when fear gnaws at your confidence.
- Believe a pearl of great value is waiting for you.
- Make your diving a daily practice.
- Leave distractions at the surface; keep your eyes on the prize.
- Take care of yourself, or you cannot do what you are meant to do.
- Let each dive teach you more about yourself and your work.
- Accept the grace and dignity that come with the process of diving deep.
- Savor each breath.
- Be grateful for the beauty in and around you.
- Come alive in the timelessness of the moment.
- Know that you alone are meant to do this work on this day and in this way.
- Be mindful of the elements; do not dive when the sea is in turmoil.

The amas learn to dive deep. They teach their daughters how to dive deeper and deeper. The amas turn what some would label a flaw into a gift. Women hold fat in our bodies. That natural trait that some women war against all our lives is what keeps the amas alive: having enough (but not too much) body fat protects the amas from freezing. By accepting this (to some, unappealing) trait, amas grow confident in their purpose.

What do we teach our children about the deeper rules or the spiritual principles that will carry us successfully through life and perhaps beyond?

Rise above It

My father taught me what he knew about adversity. Has anyone urged you to "rise above it" when you face troubles?

My father frequently exhorted others: "Rise above it!" I did my best as a child to follow his commands. The only way I knew to rise above was to climb.

Give Yourself a Break

When I climbed as high as I could up my favorite apple tree in Margery Sage's abandoned orchard behind our house, I could gather the fullest and warmest apple blossoms to my face to breathe in their soft, pink scent. I would snap off the loveliest branch to take home to my mother. Pink was her favorite color. During summertime hide-and-seek games, I climbed into my secret apple-tree hiding place until my friends had to call: "Ollie Ollie Oxen free!" In the autumn, by climbing I had my choice of the plumpest, reddest "sheep nose" apples.

As a person who makes a difference, what spiritual principles guide you? List those beliefs you live by that help you know what to do when you might not be sure what to do. Take time to listen to your favorite music or read literature that helps you live out these principles.

The stilts my father built for me were two tall pieces of raw wood, hammered to two short horizontal wooden blocks for my feet. To master the art of walking on stilts, I had to first figure out how to climb up onto the stilts. My stilts waited motionless on the grass until I figured out exactly how to tilt one toward me, step up on it while pushing the stilt and me forward in an arc and lifting the second stilt in the same upward arc so I could stand with both feet. I was so motivated to rise above that I practiced and practiced until the stilts and I became one. Literally uplifted, I clunked off down the road to rediscover my world from a taller and safer and freer perspective.

If I hiked high enough up the uninhabited hillside at the end of our street, above the soggy cattails, through the thick meadows, over the cascading clear little spring, higher than the white birches, I could reach the Old Oak Tree. Arching protectively over the hillside, the Old Oak Tree was my sanctuary. Resting against her broad, welcoming trunk, I could watch the Chemung River meander through the valley below. On summer days, the Chemung flowed gently as a lullaby. In the winter, the Chemung froze steely white. In the spring, the Chemung swelled, threatening to flood both the town and farmers' fields. My Old Oak Tree and I witnessed the seasons together.

I so loved my Old Oak Tree. I drew sketches on lined paper of the earthen house I would build for myself beside her and of the raft I would construct of birch to escape down the river.

But shelter was not my Old Oak Tree's only gift. Suspended from her fullest branch was a braided metal cable anchored by one white birch log at the bottom. By gathering the primitive swing back to the tree trunk and stepping up on the log, I could launch myself over the valley, swinging above the forest, the stream, the meadows, the cattails, and my fears.

"Rising above it" worked. I learned to welcome higher vantage points from which I might view my world. I gained perspective. Rising above it became my approach to troubles. My father was right: Rising up above the fray offers a way to see the world anew. Troubles can be seen in proper perspective. Hurts can be soothed by taking the long view. Insights can be gleaned by witnessing the big picture. Rising above a difficult situation is a spiritual way of understanding what matters and what does not. Each rising-above experience offers us a second chance to marvel, to see, to witness beauty up close and from a distance. This is transcendence.

When you were a child, where was your spiritual sanctuary, that place where you felt safe, soothed, relaxed, and content? Who helped you discover your pathway to this sanctuary? Each of us discovers or yearns to find that place on earth and within ourselves that is our sanctuary. Some people return to their sanctuary only during a vacation from work, by hiking a hillside or walking the beach at sunrise. Some people find sanctuary in loving relationships. Some of us find sanctuary in poetry or music that touches our soul. Even if we cannot physically go to our sanctuary, we can picture ourselves there and in so doing restore calm to our spirit.

Our sanctuary is our ultimate second chance. Each time we enter our sanctuary, we breathe more deeply and feel assured that life is good and will go on no matter what. Poet Robert Browning described sanctuary that arises from our knowing that "God's in His heaven—all's right with the world."

The Executive Function's Task: Rising above It (or Diving beneath It)

"Rising above it" is a homespun way of describing the executive function's connection to the amygdala. By taking steps to lift out of the fray, or just the pressures of the moment, we gain needed perspective. Before I mastered how to walk on stilts, I remained a child's height. If I hadn't learned to climb the apple tree, I would have missed both blossoms and the juiciest apples. If I hadn't devoted time to hiking up to my Old Oak Tree, I would not have

Comfort in Little Things

We all need a place on Earth where we feel safe, at ease, loved, and true to ourselves. Often that place is a place of beauty. Our souls need beauty. Where is your sacred place? If you can, journey to that place and let your spirit rest there. If you cannot physically get there, find a quiet place where you can recall what being in your sacred space feels like. Allow yourself to savor the feeling of standing on holy ground.

seen the seasons so wondrously unfold through the river's movement. The amygdala keeps our head down; the prefrontal cortex lifts our eyes to the horizon and beyond.

Without our prefrontal cortex, life is measured by how many tasks we complete and by nights and days crossed off the calendar. As we increase our access to our executive function, we open ourselves to wonder. We transcend the ordinary or can see the ordinary anew.

When Rising above Is Not an Option: The Invisibility Response

Some practices we learn as children place us on our pathway to a fulfilling life. Other practices hold us down. Let's look at a childhood practice that does not lift us up. Keep in mind that even unhappy survival practices offer us second chances to learn another way.

The world outside is full of wonder and beauty and learning. We have many hills to climb and skills to master, even from the youngest age. How painful it is to see children who cannot explore outside safely. If a bullet is zinging over his head or a drug deal is taking place in the alley beside the church, how can a child be free to learn?

I am forever grateful to have been somehow protected as I explored alone for hours in the forests on the hillsides. The benefit of having been neglected was that I could wander and play to my heart's content, learning and happy much of the time. But because my sanctuaries were outside of me, I could not always reach them in time.

Trouble was, what took place behind locked doors and closed curtains was the opposite of sanctuary. When violence in my family's world imploded out of control on a cold night, I couldn't run to my Old Oak Tree. I could not climb up and out to the orchard. Instead, like many children who grow up in threatening environments, I held my breath until I felt invisible.

Playing Dead, Tonic Immobility: Thanatosis

When children attempt to protect themselves by freezing in place and holding very still, while silently concentrating on not being noticed, it is called *tonic immobility* or the *thanatosis reflex*. The heartbeat slows. The blood flow slows. Children become pale and appear lifeless.

If you have seen an animal "play possum" or "play dead," you have seen this phenomenon. Stalking predators, alert for movement, pass by unmoving prey. Slowly the prey or child can emerge. After the danger passes, the child is relieved only on the surface. Her amygdala ticks on in a continuously alert state, scanning for threats. What if the predator suddenly returns? When this happens, the possibility of a second chance is pushed away by hypervigilance. Hypervigilance is scanning our environment for threats. As we focus on threats, we have difficulty rising above to see the beauty.

Immediate Benefit of Thanatosis: Long-Term Cost of Playing Dead

The "playing possum" response nonetheless serves a purpose. It protects children. Perhaps you have known a child who was unnoticeable on the playground or in the classroom until you took a head count. "Oh, there's Laura! She's so quiet I forgot she was in school today." Laura might need to be invisible at home or in the presence of a dangerous person. She is acting in a way that keeps her out of harm's way and demonstrating what she has learned to do to survive: hide until she is safe.

Unlike the freeing practice of rising above it, the tonic immobility survival response freezes our development. The amygdala triggers this "play dead" response, which is a form of flight. The child doesn't decide to become invisible. She freezes. The child's spirit and happiness fly away while her body freezes to protect itself. She is still frighteningly vulnerable. As a practice, invisibility sometimes backfires. The child is caught. Post-traumatic stress disorder (PTSD) is often the consequence.

What Produces PTSD in Children?

Just one traumatic experience can produce post-traumatic stress disorder. Far too many children were traumatized by watching the World Trade Center towers collapse, as the horror continuously looped on television channels. The children in Newtown, Connecticut, who otherwise may have led peaceful lives, lost that sense of internal peace when the shooter entered their school. When the devastating tornado hit the schools in Moore, Oklahoma, children's safety was deeply shaken. These single events can trigger PTSD.

When children are continuously in danger, their "gears get stripped" by having too much cortisol in their system. Sadly, in these cases PTSD is a predictable outcome. Children who go through the foster care system, moving from one placement to another, can be retraumatized by each move. Each removal from a home can reactivate the original abandonment they felt when they were first taken from their original home. PTSD is virtually unavoidable.

Don't We All Play Dead at Some Point?

Although the invisibility response may sound extreme, it is something we all use at some point or another. We look down to avoid eye contact. We pretend to be engaged at work when we are not. We deny to ourselves that we are under siege or unhappy. We metaphorically hold our breath until the threat passes.

Whether we are in danger of being called out publicly or being forced to face a conflict we would rather avoid, we can attempt to be invisible. When we are invisible or in denial, we are all about survival. Survival is too rudimentary for transcendence. We exist in the cellar of Maslow's hierarchy.

Rising above conflicts and stressors in the moment is difficult. And yet that's where freedom lies. Freedom is a lifelong quest. Stressors don't quit. However, our relationships with stressors can change. Having dedicated a year to discovering the spirituality of second chances, I can trace my progress on learning to rise above internally without needing to escape externally.

When I became an adult with responsibilities, I began to see other meanings of "Rise above it." Shall we see if you believe we can rise above even the heaviest of burdens? Consider your responsibilities and stressors. In fact, take this moment to list them one by one:

* For whom and for what are you responsible?
* What are the stressors in your life, including the small as well as the large ones?

Are you tired yet? Honestly, I don't want to take time to write my list! I know it all too well, and while writing it down, I would feel as if I were taking time away from those responsibilities. Stepping back from the stressors is hard. Stepping back requires that I pull out of the amygdala's unconscious control into the executive function's conscious state.

This chapter is about finding transcendence, or "rising above" the mundane into the extraordinary. Our spirits quest for meaning. Our minds overheat without cooling perspective. We need a soothing friend, and for many of us, that friend is spirituality.

Spirituality emerges from crucible experiences, those trials that throw us into the fire or the freezing waters. We all have crucible moments. Our way of facing those moments defines who we are and who we can become.

Spirituality: What Is It?

Human beings yearn for transcendence. We seek a life of meaning and fulfillment. As educators, we are on Earth to make a difference. We seek ways to make sense of why we are given losses and confronted with injustices. We aim to leave the world a better place for our children and their children. Transcendence is an educator's legacy: as we give back, so shall our students pay it forward.

Spirituality is this desire to live a meaningful and fulfilling life, so we can come to the end of our lives without fear or regret. As Maya Angelou reminds us, "I've learned that people will forget what you said, people will forget what you did, but people will never forget how you made them feel."

Keep in mind that spirituality and religion are not necessarily the same. Religious institutions and beliefs provide pathways and principles that guide us as we try to live our lives according to a deity's plan. A deity or sacred leader has different names (God, Jesus, Allah, Yahweh, Muhammad, Great Spirit, Buddha, the Universe) in different religions. For some people, religion is their spiritual path. For others, the Twelve Steps of recovery, based on William James's *The Varieties of Religious Experience*, provide another pathway.

Let me be clear: I respect everybody's choice to follow a religion or to find their own path, do some of both, or be nonreligious. When I refer to spirituality in the pages of this book, however, I am referring to our human quest for a meaningful life and, in particular, our quest as educators to make a difference in people's lives for the better, one child at a time.

Howard Gardner, who described "multiple intelligences" in his book *Frames of Mind*, helps establish our commitment to social-emotional development. In his book, we can read about the variety of other intelligences, from kinesthetic to artistic. What has received far less attention is Gardner's more recent work on spiritual intelligence, *Intelligence Reframed* (1999).

Like Gardner, Maslow places spirituality at the top of his hierarchy of human needs. Maslow also views spirituality as the human quest to find meaning. In my experience, almost every educator I meet has a passion for going deeper to reach each child and to help that child find her path. In accompanying each child, we walk farther down our spiritual path. We transcend together.

Throughout this book on second chances, we puzzle and work through or simply enjoy the process of finding meaning in ordinary moments. In each moment, as we are offered a second chance, we are also offered a way to climb farther up our path spiritually. You are always in charge of what you seek to discover. The choice is yours to act or not act, reflect upon or move on.

The amas' tradition inspired me to draft a list of spiritual principles that I learned from their story. Each of us has a story. This book embodies my learning so far about spiritual principles. What would your book say about the spiritual principles you have gleaned from living your life, especially as an educator?

Soothed by the comfort of little things, we can find our way to a deeper, holier place. We are on the road to reclaiming our birthright to joy. We always deserve love. We always deserve a second chance.

Reflection Questions

1. The amas dive deep for the treasure of a rare pearl. As a child, I climbed an apple tree, walked atop stilts, and climbed up the hillside to rest beside the Old Oak Tree. Do you have a practice you use to find deeper meaning or at least clearer perspective? If so, what are you transcending, and what is the pearl?

2. Can you recall the names or faces of children who were less visible (or even invisible) than others? What caused you not to notice this child? If you got a chance to get to know this child better, what did you discern was the reason the child had learned to become invisible? As an adult, do you face situations in which you would prefer to be invisible? When we are invisible to others, do we become invisible to ourselves?

3. What helps you "rise above" situations that would otherwise pull you down? When you face trials, do you take a spiritual path up and out of

the trouble? What spiritual principles have you learned in the process? Provide an example of a time you were able to rise above a difficult and demanding challenge.

4. Can you sense and describe, in any way, what it's like for you to transition from the unconscious (autonomic system) into more consciousness? What helps you succeed in this quest?

5. What does spirituality mean to you, and how does your spirituality help you as an educator? Is your spirituality the same as, akin to, or not connected at all to religion? Where do you go to feel spiritually connected, at home, or at peace? Are you able to create such spaces at work?

Chapter 8

Failure, the Crucible for Second Chances
It's Not What You Did to Fail, It's What You Do Next

When you make a mistake; when you fail: You are not a failure; you are not a mistake. You are a human being with a second chance.

Silly Me

What did you say to yourself the last time you failed at something that mattered to you? Or the last time you made a mistake?

My son, Nick, who stumbled at a lot of things he wanted to do, taught me a life lesson. As a four-year-old, when he missed his mark. Nick would shrug his shoulders, lean his head to the side, smile a little, and then say, "Silly me."

Nick's gentle "Silly me" opened the door to a second chance. He could try another approach or let go and move on. After months of working on the challenge to "use his words" instead of biting a classmate in frustration, Nick created words that worked for him. "Silly me" helped Nick lighten up. He could save face, which mattered to him, especially as a child diagnosed with pervasive developmental delays. "Silly me" was so much more effective for him than acting out.

These same words now work for me. I know I'm going to get through my latest (otherwise embarrassing) mistake when I hear myself say, "Silly me." Love you, Nick.

Proclamations of Failure

What do you hear adults say to themselves when they fail?

It breaks my heart when I hear many educators put themselves down with statements like "Stupid me!" or "How dumb can I get?" We have so many ways to curse ourselves.

Think about what cursing means. Back in the day, to curse meant to cast a negative "spell." Today, cursing still amounts to wishing harm on ourselves or others. Cursing is a proclamation of our inadequacy. We wound our esteem each time we curse ourselves. Our brains take our words seriously.

Children teach us so much. Nick taught me that I have a choice. What I said to myself in the past when I failed does not have to be what I say to myself today. With practice, I am replacing self-condemnation with the uplifting words "Silly me." Like my son, I can shrug my shoulders, smile a little, lift my eyebrows, tilt my head to the side, and eventually find another path.

Opportunities for Second Chances

I have had so many opportunities to practice Nick's "Silly me" technique in my life. Believe me, I have made explosive mistakes. I have failed dismally. I have tried all the usual tactics to vamoose from the scene of my crimes. Have you used any of these tactics to avoid feeling like a failure?

* denial
* cover-up
* telling lies
* shifting the blame elsewhere
* faking an apology
* arguing you were right to do what you did
* running away
* beating yourself up
* calling yourself names
* letting a shame attack overtake you

- going numb
- feeling like nuclear waste
- feeling hopelessly unworthy

I'm sure more tactics will present themselves to me as options. My mind never gives up on self-protection.

Admitting I have failed can be so painful, I forget I can get through the failure. I forget I can breathe. I forget I have a second chance. My old pal the amygdala feels threatened and stands ready to tell me how to survive. I am the one who needs to invoke my executive function. In partnership with the amygdala's prodding, the executive function can help me regain generosity of spirit. Generosity of spirit goes both ways: to others and back to my hurting self.

Truth to tell, I know none of these defensive tactics works. Or works for long. Each tactic takes me down a bumpy dirt road, away from the truth. Away from transcendence. Covering up failure is hard work: I have to remember what lie I told to whom and when. It's exhausting. Why not acknowledge my failure and make amends?

I know all this. But I also know that the urge to escape my failures is a muscular bully, hard to deny, and certainly not something I can reason with. So, I begin the predictable conversation with myself.

The Internal Medieval Morality Play

In the Middle Ages, before television and movie theaters, morality plays were the go-to form of entertainment. A traveling band of players (actors and musicians) would trek from town to town, like one of today's rock bands. The morality players would construct a stage with a trapdoor through which wrongdoers could be banished to the pits of hell. Behind the curtain at the back of the stage hid the sound effects folk, ready to create thunder and the *clip-clop* sound of horses' hooves.

Morality plays were all about good winning over evil. Everyone knew the stories that would be told, just as we can predict the conversations we will have with ourselves when we mess up. Perhaps because the events were so familiar, the townspeople could laugh at themselves and their foibles. Of course, a few bawdy characters and some friendly, horned devils gave "pop" to the laughter.

As you read through the plot of one of my familiar internal morality plays, if you wish, ask yourself, do I have a morality play in my repertoire too?

Bully versus Conscience: Who Will Win the Battle?

The Bully of Fear threatens: "If you don't go along with me to cover this up, I'll trash you with the worst shame attack of your life. You know I can make you feel like bathtub scum, worthless, lower than dirt. I'll call you a Failure. I'll say you are a Mistake. You don't want to go there, do you?"

Conscience nips at my heels until I pay attention.

Conscience reminds me: "Just do it. Just take responsibility for what you did. Remember you're human. Humans make mistakes. Humans fail. Apologize. Make things right. I know you can. Remember, you don't have to take responsibility for more than what you have done. Keep it simple. I'll help you get through this like I always have. You will walk taller again."

What a medieval drama I can run in my head!

I tell you these things because I have come to believe that honesty is the simplest and most direct approach with myself and others. Once I have taken responsibility, I can change my ways and make amends to put things right. I have come to see that failure isn't what defines me, what I do after I fail is how I define myself.

I tell you these things because I want you to know that even though I may look like I have it together, I am no Ms. Goody Two-shoes and no stranger to failure. Perhaps this is why second chances are so powerful for me.

Why Failure Is Hard to Admit

"You ought to be ashamed of yourself." Have you heard or said that?

"You ought to feel so bad about yourself that you feel worthless." That's the message: unworthiness. You are a failure. Who wants to hear or admit to that?

Guess what? When we are told our behavior is shameful, we can fall prey to a debilitating shame attack. The amygdala will drag us down into self-hatred. Over and over again, we will recall our failure. Each time we recall the failure, we feel awful about ourselves. We can stay down in that dark cellar until we have sufficiently done penance. Tail between our legs, self-esteem banished, we can emerge no longer believing in ourselves. Failure defines us as outcasts.

Shame is a debilitating emotion. It takes hostages. It banishes the hope of a second chance.

Shame trashes our perspective. Guilt is a different emotion. It is a more reflective part of our conscience. Guilt is far more pragmatic: "You made a mistake? You failed? Okay, that's how you learn. Take responsibility, change your behavior, apologize, and get on with your life." Guilt tempers our character for the better. Shame destroys character and labels us incurable. If you had a choice, which would you choose: shame or guilt?

What do you mean, I can choose? Doesn't shame inflict itself on my spirit whether I choose to feel ashamed of myself or not?

Sure, shame is always ready to overtake us. The amygdala is always scanning the environment for threats. When shame takes over, I take myself out of the action to "lick my wounds." In that curious way, shame attacks accomplish an amygdala function: flight. Running from the solution to the problem keeps our amygdala pumping adrenaline or cortisol. We feel worse and worse. Where's the choice in that?

Our executive function is always ready to help us out of an amygdala hijack. Little ways can free us. Remember the tools you identified and read about in chapter 4: breathe, count from ten backwards, pray, recite your favorite saying, sing your favorite song to yourself. Shame attacks are weakened by any of these tools. With the help of our prefrontal cortex, we can choose to transition from perseveration to perspective. In fact, with the help of our spiritual principles (chapter 7), we can transcend shame.

Like panic attacks, shame attacks sucker punch our spirit. Guilt challenges our spirit to own up to our shortcomings, learn, change, and move on. Between guilt and shame, choose guilt. "Have dignity, you understand me? Choose dignity," advises a character in Saul Bellow's appropriately titled book *The Victim* (120). Shame attacks turn us into victims; choosing dignity restores our soul.

Remember the spiritual lessons from the amas, the pearl fishers? One of those pearl-like principles is, "Let each dive teach you more about yourself and your work."

What is a second chance if not another opportunity to learn? As we learn, we change. As we change, we are offered the opportunity to ease up on ourselves. Judging myself and others snatches me directly out of the moment and plops me down in a cow pasture where bulls are waiting. Children learn. Educators learn. We are educators. We can learn to be gentle with ourselves.

So You've Made a Mistake—What Do You Do Next?

Even when we feel we are at our worst, we have choices. Viktor Frankl, author of *Man's Search for Meaning* (1959), lost his wife and young son in a Nazi concentration camp. Heartsick, but soldiering on, Frankl questioned why some people maintain resilience in even the darkest of times while others give up. He concluded, "Everything can be taken from a man but one thing: the last of the human freedoms—to choose one's attitude in any given set of circumstances, to choose one's own way" (66). Choosing one's own way is choosing a second chance.

Frankl's insight offers us perspective on many difficult situations. Some people berate themselves, saying, "If I make a mistake, I am a mistake." Frankl points us in another direction: When I make a mistake, what do I do next? Perhaps instead of focusing on beating ourselves up, we could choose to make things better. In this way, we can find comfort in little things and move on.

Give Yourself a Break

Name one mistake you have made; but, more importantly, remind yourself: "What life lessons did I learn from that experience? How did that failure/mistake help me grow?"

What Can I Do When I Know I Am Wrong?

This process is direct and achievable and always results in a second chance for ourselves and all others around us. Here are the steps:

1. Ask yourself, "What have I done that conflicts with my personal and professional standards and with my spiritual principles?"
2. Be concrete and factual with yourself: Was the mistake what you did? What you said? What you didn't do or say?
3. Separate your responsibility from the responsibility of others; beware of taking on what is another person's responsibility.
4. Decide what you will do to make things right.
5. Apologize authentically (see tips later in this chapter for how to apologize effectively).
6. Explain what you will do to make the other person or situation whole.
7. Change your behavior: do what you say you will do.

8. Observe and acknowledge your change of heart; articulate to yourself what you have learned from this failure.

9. Notice where you are: What second chance has owning up to this challenge given you? Take that chance.

Magic Words

My son and daughter learned early on that when I reminded them to use their "magic words," I hoped they would remember to say either "Thank you" or "I'm sorry," depending on the situation. I was especially grateful when Nick wouldn't roll his eyes or scowl when he said "I'm sorry." Who hasn't heard an "I'm sorry" that really meant "I am anything but sorry"? An authentic apology can be the balm of Gilead, soothing wounded souls. A forced apology, as my mother used to say, "rubs salt in the wound." Teacher Maggie in chapter 2 did not force little Valerie to say "I am sorry" before the child was ready. Instead, the teacher offered the child another way to set things right: offer help to another person who is hurting.

An authentic apology can have healing results that feel at times like magic. Resentments don't form; sides don't have to be taken. Acceptance sets in even before forgiveness. To be authentic, believable, and healing when making an apology, make your apology:

- from the heart;
- real, sincere, and authentic;
- timely, given as soon as possible after the mistake is made;
- followed by a change of behavior as well as and a change in heart;
- restorative to the persons harmed, making them as whole again as possible; and
- a clear signal that the same mistake will not be made again.

Let's apply these insights on how to apologize to a case study that comes out of my own experience.

CASE STUDY: *Holly Elissa's Foot-in-Mouth Syndrome*

Ready to present a workshop on "Partnering with Families That Push Your Buttons," trainer Holly Elissa walks around to greet as many of the participants in the session as she can. When she notices a woman in the front row whose large belly surely indicates a pregnancy, Holly Elissa asks, "When's your baby due?" The room becomes silent. The woman declares stiffly, "I am not pregnant."

If you were Holly Elissa in that situation, what would you do and/or say in the moment?

Let's apply the steps:

1. Ask yourself: What have I done that is wrong (according to my personal and professional standards)? Answer: *I labeled a person incorrectly. I disrespected her boundaries. I inappropriately called attention to her in public. I said something hurtful.*

2. Be concrete and factual with yourself: Was the mistake what you did? What you said? What you didn't do or say? Answer: *I told a woman she was pregnant without checking the facts. I did this in a public setting.*

3. Separate your responsibility from the responsibility of others; beware of taking on what is another person's responsibility. Answer: *I am responsible for what I said, for apologizing immediately, for learning from my mistake, and for doing what I can to help the rest of the group bounce back from witnessing my inappropriate behavior.*

4. Decide what you will do to make things right. Answer: *I will apologize immediately, first to the person and then to the group.*

5. Apologize authentically. Answer: to the individual: *"I am so sorry for what I said. My comment was inconsiderate and inappropriate."* To the group (who heard what I said): *"I apologize for making an inappropriate remark. I feel very bad about what I said. I will do all I can to present this workshop in a way that helps us all move on from my mistake."*

6. Determine what you will do to make the other person or situation whole. Answer: *1. I will not make another flippant remark, especially on the assumption that someone is pregnant. 2. I will conduct the workshop professionally and positively.*

7. Change your behavior: do what you determine to do. Answer: *I act as I committed myself to act in number 6. What remains is for me to learn from this mistake.*

8. Observe and acknowledge your change of heart; articulate to yourself what this failure has taught you. Answer: *Check out assumptions before saying something, especially in front of others, and especially about possible pregnancy.*

9. Notice where you are: What second chance has owning up to this challenge given you? Agree to take that chance. Answer: *I share this with others, saying what I did and what I learned. My honesty frequently helps others accept and talk about their mistakes and what they learned.*

Here's something else I've learned from apologizing: The sooner I apologize, the better. The sooner I take responsibility for my actions, the more believable my apology. The longer I hold the apology inside me, the less I can breathe freely. Did I have a shame attack when I asked this woman when her baby was due? Yes, a very red-faced, I-want-to-disappear-off-the-face-of-the-earth! shame attack. Was the shame attack abated when I apologized to her and to the group? Yes.

I admit I relived that shame attack as I drove back to my office. I relived it the first and the second and the third time I talked about it. However, each time I talked about my mistake, I took time to ask if anyone else had done the same (or a similar) thing. Floodgates opened. Other trainers had made the same mistake. Other people had made similar mistakes. Everyone had something to share. And there it was. In the sharing came a second chance for all of us.

In the sharing came relief, learning, hope, forgiveness, and energy for change. That's the way second chances work. Second chances are a spiritual route. Every time we say yes to giving or taking a second chance, we uplift others and ourselves to live more freely, less burdened by "shoulds" (I should have done this; I should have said that). In fact, when I turn a "should" into a "did it," the "should" loses its power to shame. The "should" flies back into my personal code of professional responsibility, ready for me to act on my principles again. As the amas remind me, take care of yourself or you cannot do what you are meant to do.

When to Apologize

Barbara Kellerman, in her 2006 *Harvard Business Review* article "When Should a Leader Apologize and When Not," lays out a useful checklist for how to decide whether to apologize. In addition, she offers guidance on how to apologize. Kellerman cautions us to take responsibility for our actions while making sure we don't take on the mistakes of others. Here are the standards by which to judge when an apology is necessary. An apology is appropriate when:

To listen to my conversation with Barbara Kellerman, "When and How to Say 'I Was Wrong,'" go to www.bamradionetwork.com, and type "Barbara Kellerman" into the search box.

- we have failed in our responsibility to do what we said we would or what we should have done;
- we are the one responsible (rather than "taking the fall" for others);
- we feel accountable for our actions/inaction;
- we are willing to take responsibility and make necessary changes to set the situation right; and
- we have checked with our attorneys to make sure an apology will not adversely affect legal action.

If a lawsuit or other disciplinary action may follow, we would be smart to consult with our attorney. Doing this isn't a way of avoiding taking responsibility. Checking with an attorney helps us know the steps we need to take to remedy this situation and prevent others like it.

How to Apologize

- Apologize authentically—only if you mean it.
- Apologize as soon after the event as possible.
- Apologize directly to the person harmed.
- Apologize publicly if appropriate.
- State what you did wrong, how you feel about what you did or said, and how you will make things right.
- Change your behavior: walk the talk.
- Take action to set things right.
- Don't go back on your promise: make the change part of who you are.

How Others Feel about Us When We Apologize

Gender seems to affect how we feel about apologizing. "Apologies are less expected from managers and males than from subordinates and females, and the less expected they are, the greater their effectiveness," note Tamar Walfisch and colleagues (Walfisch, Van Dijk, and Kark 2013, 1446), who conducted a study on gender's impact on how we give and receive apologies. Although this Israeli study suggests that women's apologies will have less power then men's, another conclusion might be: Don't apologize unless you mean it, and prove that you mean it. A woman who is true to her word and makes a behavior change that aligns with her apology will be respected in her organization by both women and men.

While noting also that apologizing lowers our blood pressure, in her article "The Power of Apology," Beverly Engel (2002) shares these interpersonal positive effects of apologizing:

- A person who has been harmed feels emotional healing when he is acknowledged by the wrongdoer.
- When we receive an apology, we no longer perceive the wrongdoer as a personal threat.
- An apology helps us move past our anger and prevents us from being stuck in the past.
- An apology opens the door to forgiveness by allowing us to have empathy for the wrongdoer.
- An apology has the power to humble even the most arrogant person.
- Apologizing keeps us connected.

In most of the studies I reviewed, apologizing is seen as an offer to rebuild a relationship. Sounds like another way to describe a second chance.

When You Can't Make Amends to the Person Directly

To read an abstract of Walfisch, Van Dijk, and Kark's study "Do You Really Expect Me to Apologize? The Impact of Status and Gender on the Effectiveness of an Apology in the Workplace," go to www.academia.edu, sign up, and search for the authors' name and the title of the study.

In some situations, apologizing to the person affected by our mistake is not a possibility. Perhaps the person dies. Perhaps the person refuses to talk with us. In these cases, where making a direct apology is not an option, we still need to make an apology. A major function of apologizing is to heal ourselves.

Sure, we hope the person harmed is restored or made whole. However, we can never change another person. That other person has to choose whether she will allow us to reach her. When another person rejects my apology, I can go to a deeper place to find a second chance. Each jagged moment reminds me that optimism is always an option. It's no surprise that wherever I live, one of the first things I do is plant bulbs for the spring and seeds for the summer.

Hope reminds me: I am the one who can choose to change. I can choose to take different action. I can change my attitude. This is possible regardless of the other person's response (or nonresponse). This is where paying it forward works. I have choices. I can be of service to another individual who is hurting. I can be of service to the community. I can put my apology in action. I can change my ways.

For example, if the woman whom I called pregnant left the session and refused to talk with me, I could still make amends to the other participants. I can carry and implement my learning into all my future interactions. The person to whom I apologized (or who refused my apology) gets to choose what she will accept. I cannot make this decision for that person. However, I can decide to change myself. This second chance is always available. This second chance makes things better.

Why an Apology Trumps Beating Yourself Up

Can feeling guilty ever be a selfish act? Although this may sound counter-intuitive, I believe the answer is yes. When I allow my energy to be sapped by guilt, I have little energy left for my work. I can't think of others if I am preoccupied with my own worries. For sure, I can't improve my behavior unless I can "get over myself" first.

Roger Neugebauer, in his Exchange Everyday e-mail notifications, sends insights and tidbits of information that he believes will be helpful to early childhood professionals. Here is one of Neugebauer's e-mails:

A director in New Jersey once told me, "Guilt is a selfish emotion." I was stunned! I always thought feeling guilty was the first step toward accepting responsibility for what I need to change. For that director, prolonged guilty feelings block her from taking action to make changes for the better. Guilt is "all about me" and is paralyzing. In that case, I came to see her point. As Wayne Dyer, author and motivational speaker, observes, "Worry is an attempt to control the future. Guilt is an attempt to control the past." Perspective is a director's best friend (Bruno 2012).

Creating a Culture of Second Chances

Making amends can be difficult. Courage and humility are required for a true apology. Courage is choosing to do the right thing, regardless of the external and internal pressures not to take action. Beating ourselves up and feeling guilty can be far easier than acting courageously.

Humility is accepting our "perfectly imperfect" selves. I picture humility as the melting of my ego: my stubbornness and my pride melt down to make room for me to act more kindly. Every time I make amends rather than wallow in guilt, I feel freer within myself and more hopeful about the world. Does that make sense?

Our path eases up a little when we make a sincere apology for our misdoing. The path truly eases up when we relax our egos, forgive ourselves, learn something in the process, and regain our sense of humor. Humor is not only a "saving grace," humor is the threshold to a second chance.

Reflection Questions

1. Take another look at Lyra's case study in chapter 2. What do you think Lyra could say and do to make things right with Winston's family and everyone else (including herself) who has been harmed by her action/inaction?

    To whom does Lyra need to apologize?

    What would she need to say to each person?

    Does she need to make any amends to herself?

    What actions can Lyra take to let herself and others know that her apology is real?

    If her apologies are not accepted by others, what can Lyra do?

Comfort in Little Things

Some of us never received the apologies we deserve. That failure on the part of the other person to accept responsibility for causing us harm can leave a wound. Imagine that the person is now apologizing to you. Write down the words that you hear. Little by little release yourself from waiting any longer for the other person to set things right. That other person has her own wounds. You have the power to forgive and move on.

What's likely going on beneath the surface with Lyra's amygdala and prefrontal cortex?

What are the possible second chances waiting for Lyra to take (and to give)?

How would the "notice where you are" practice help Lyra?

2. Recall apologies you have either given or received. What distinguished between a believable apology and one that felt like a hollow gesture? Do some people make apologizing to them easy and other people make apologizing almost impossible? For whom do you make the apology (yourself, the other person, or both of you)?

3. Foot-in-the-mouth syndrome: Have you ever had this? What happened? What did you do in the moment? What did you learn from that experience?

4. Do you think gender makes a difference when it comes to apologies? Do you agree that a man's apology is more potent than a woman's? What do children who observe adults learn about the "maleness" or "femaleness" of apologizing? What would we like children to learn?

5. What are the alternatives to insisting that a child apologize in the moment? Recall a time when you observed a child being forced to apologize. What did you notice about that child's response? What did the child learn, do you think, from the forced apology?

6. Consider how you could apply the theories and strategies in this chapter to case studies in earlier chapters: What could director Miranda in chapter 5 say to her assistant director? How could Trixie Marie, the difficult teacher in chapter 4, change her pathway by making an honest apology to her director, Yalena?

Chapter 9

 ## Second Chance Denied

When the Door Is Slammed in Your Face, Where Can You Turn?

People deal too much with the negative, with what is wrong. . . .
Why not try to see positive things, to just touch those things and
make them bloom?—*Thich Nhat Hanh*

When is the last time you were judged unfairly? What were you accused of, or how were you misperceived? Were you labeled? Stereotyped? How did you feel then, and how do you feel now just recalling that time? What did you learn from that experience of being judged? Here's how I felt:

Rejection. Ouch! Being eliminated. Ouch! Being shunned. Ouch! Being discriminated against. Ouch! Facing injustice. Ouch! Not being seen or heard. Ouch! Being denied a second chance. Ouch.

These things hurt. Being judged, especially when the judgment is unfair, is a direct strike through our spirit. No one wants to hear he is a failure, or unacceptable, or unlovable. Feeling unworthy dyes everything blood red. Being judged hurts, and it can also make us angry. Being negatively judged most always feels unfair and shovels the dirt of shame on our already vulnerable self-concept.

A friend told me she's learned that the worst thing she can do when she's been judged negatively is to hold resentment toward the person making the judgment. Resentment, she said, overtakes her heart with tentacles. When she allows herself to feel resentment, she surrenders her freedom to

Believe nothing just because someone else believes it. But believe only what you yourself test and judge to be true. —Buddha

her judger. My friend is black. She has faced a lifetime of negative judgment, spoken and unspoken. I learn from her.

We know these things. But can we ease up on judging others and ourselves? According to the Myers-Briggs Type Indicator, 55 percent of Americans are inclined to quickly judge people and situations. If you are in this majority, you are likely dedicated to getting the job done, getting it done correctly, finishing ahead of time, and you might not always be patient with people who aren't similarly inclined. The remaining 45 percent of Americans are less inclined to judge and more likely to accept different styles, including last-minute approaches and imperfect paperwork (Myers et al. 1998).

Being in the minority means you will be judged by the majority. Less-judgmental people will feel the effects of negative judgments, and those who are in the education profession are likely to take those judgments personally. People who are not as inclined to make quick judgments themselves can, out of self-defense, negatively label the majority culture as a group of uptight, controlling perfectionists.

Do we have a standoff? You might think so if you heard the number of times a teacher asks to be reassigned to work with a different team teacher because of this very same "personality conflict." When one teacher labels another teacher a slob, the labeler sets herself up for being labeled a control freak. Ouch again.

When doors slam and lock in our face, second chances seem as exiled as we are.

Learning from Past Experiences

In this response to my post number six, "Untying Myself," on my blog *Share Your Stories*, reader Michelle Manganaro wrote the following reply about learning from past mistakes and giving yourself a second chance. See if you can relate to what she has to say.

When I was in college, I couldn't wait to be married and have children. As a result, I settled down with [a] boy from my hometown who seemed mature and ready. The relationship lasted almost ten years but ended abruptly with news of his affair; heartbreaking, of course.

A year later I began a long-term relationship with a man, who finally said to me, "I am paying for all of your ex's mistakes." Apparently his expression of love for me was consistently met with my sarcasm; I cared for him but could not believe or trust he truly cared for me. Heartbreaking, actually.

Because I had been lied to and mistreated (and for such a long period—essentially the decade called my 20s), the truth sent me through the stages of mourning. During my early 30s, it was hard for me to believe that someone could love or care about me; and actually, really mean it.

How might this apply to professional settings? It's an interpersonal thing actually. In my nineteenth year as a director among a small and changing group of professional educators, there have been many staff come and go (or stay) who had been burnt by a prior boss. Forming a relationship with me that was going to be any different than that was going to take two ingredients: desire and effort. If they didn't have the desire, it was going to become my job. Effort would be a two-way street.

I wish I'd known then, what I know now. Second chance? Well I am still a Director and relationship building is my best friend. [...] I have to give myself a little credit though—my critics (and I always had them, still do) would often say that I was a "softie" and that I was always given too many chances. One leader in the making often took her turn on the playground "soapbox" to say things like "well I would have a three strikes policy" and fire people who didn't follow the rules. I like to think I have had a more humane approach over the years that has allowed me to comfortably sleep at night. That said, having too many cooks in the kitchen is how I prefer to lead the school—cooperative and team-based, I rarely need to make a unilateral decision.

As I reflect within my own skin, I realize also that my own perceptions of trust and relationship-building with staff also play a role at work; I have to realize that my own feelings of doubt can interfere with the employee-employer relationship. And boy have I had a good amount of people over the years. Turnover was a major obstacle in the early 90s. Even now, with a family-like staff group of twenty teachers and the average length of service being nine to ten years, I am learning that there is a fundamental value with/for second chances.

On a personal note, that second romantic relationship from my early 30s that I mentioned . . . well it ended due to a hidden substance abuse issue; it became one emotional rollercoaster I simple could not ride anymore. Heartbreaking. Not to worry though, at age forty-three, I am entering the sixth year with a honey that is the best honey I've ever known. When I met him I thought he was a video game playing twenty-eight-year-old. Turns out he was a very young-looking divorced parent and that the journeys we've had are almost a mirror image of one another. The best part? Even after six years, he doesn't mind reassuring me every day that he "really does" love me. Good thing I gave the "video game playing twenty-eight-year-old" a second chance. :)

—Michelle Manganaro, October 8, 2014

Why Are Human Beings So Judgmental?

For years, educators have been encouraging acceptance: accept children and families as they are; work with them where they are. Find qualities to build upon and appreciate. The Strengthening Families Program model, run by the Substance Abuse and Mental Health Services Administration, is all about looking for and building on strengths. Its goal is to partner with families, connecting strength with strength.

The "deficit" model, in comparison, assumes people are lacking and need to be fixed. The deficit model allows judgments about inadequacies and prescribes measures to correct the deficits.

In the end these things matter most: How well did you love? How fully did you love? How deeply did you learn to let go?
—Buddha

Years ago, Head Start introduced a program review instrument called the Prism Model. Some of us called Prism "prison," because it locked evaluators into naming deficits without identifying assets. When Prism evaluators showed up, their job was to look for faults. Strengths were not to be named, and as a result, program directors began to feel less hopeful about their capacity to make positive change. Mention Prism to a Head Start veteran, and you're sure to hear stories of the problems caused when the instrument used to measure success focuses only on the negative.

Why do we judge others? What does judging accomplish?

- Standards for performance are upheld.

- Problems are identified so they can be addressed.

- Inappropriate behavior is labeled so alternatives can be presented.

- Harmful acts have consequences.

- Harmful people are removed from where they cause harm (if they can't improve).

People have a hard time letting go of their suffering. Out of a fear of the unknown, they prefer suffering that is familiar.
—Thich Nhat Hanh

These are all practical points. However, the deeper reason we judge others (and ourselves) is fear. We fear that we will lose control or that things around us will career out of control.

From a fearful stance, we label others (and/or ourselves) as lacking. We label others to keep ourselves safe. We label colleague Angela unfriendly; that way, we don't have to feel rejected by her. We label parents as not spending enough time with their children. Judging parents allows us to distance ourselves from having to engage with them fully as partners. If parents are judged as inadequate, we are freer to work with the child on our own, without having to do the work of forging a partnership.

Judgments become "self-fulfilling prophecies." We live up (or down) to the judgment we have made about ourselves. We might judge ourselves incapable of giving a presentation to a large group or not smart enough to go back to school to get that degree, be it an associate's or doctorate or Child Development Associate (CDA) credential. We might judge another as condescending or stubborn, loud or shy. As judgments morph into expectations, we start to believe our judgments are the gospel truth.

As we judge ourselves, we limit our options. We may even fear our own power or fear using it. In that case, we lessen our ability to make a difference.

Why do we fear our own power? If we believe in ourselves, we would have so much to accomplish and to be. If we don't believe in our power? We are less likely to disappoint ourselves and others. Aim low, get by. Aim high, fall hard. Confronting our own judgments is hard and takes courage. Go back to writing with your opposite hand to feel the challenge of making even a tiny change.

When I root my decisions in fear, I survive at best. I shut out second chances. Second chances require courage. Courage requires openness to change. Courage requires me to turn away from judgment and into possibility.

Courage: Saying Yes to a Second Chance and No to Fear

What is courage and how can we get ourselves some of it? Are some of us naturally courageous and the rest of us timid? Are we courageous about some things, like protecting our children, and timid about others, like standing up for ourselves?

Courage is stepping into the darkness with hope and conviction that you will find light. Courage is stepping up to do the right thing, regardless of consequences to ourselves.

For ethics and character expert Gus Lee, courage is doing the right thing, taking action that will make the greatest difference in the long run, all without holding back in fear of what might happen to you as a result. Lee says, we can choose to do:

- what will make us look good;
- the politically expedient thing; or
- that which will do the greatest good in the long run (Lee and Couras, "Do You Have the Courage to Be an Effective Educational Leader?").

Lee's early years were tough. Born in China and partially blind, Lee was raised in a black neighborhood by an unappreciative father after his mother died. Lee had no one to help him. Then, two people gave Lee a second chance. His teacher drove all the way to Lee's house to speak with his father. That teacher confronted Lee's father about not getting glasses for him. Lee was astounded that someone stood up for him. The other person who gave Lee a second chance was a strong kid from the 'hood, who offered to teach Lee how to fight back. Lee was a little guy, but with his new friend's encouragement he studied boxing until he could defend himself. That strong kid from the 'hood became a doctor. Lee became a professor at West Point. Three stories in courage: a kind teacher, a true friend, and a bullied child who fought back. One heartfelt lesson: Courage is in your heart, no matter how beaten down you have been. I know this. Give yourself a second chance to be courageous.

Remember our Lyra who hated herself for allowing a child to be hurt while Lyra was texting? What acts of courage could Lyra take now that might begin to make a world of difference to others and to herself? Often the toughest person to stand up for is yourself. That takes courage.

Faith is a bird that feels dawn breaking and sings while it is still dark. — Rabindranath Tagore

When the Door Slams in Your Face and a Second Chance Is Denied

If you are denied a second chance, what can you do? Judgments can be harsh enough to be permanent. Let's consider that dynamic to see if second chances might be possible, even in extreme circumstances.

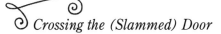
Crossing the (Slammed) Door

Although we rarely choose to separate ourselves from other people with tall stone walls, we can bump against the rock-hard and permanent barriers others erect. These walls appear too high to climb and too far-reaching to walk around. And even if we were to find a way over the wall, we wouldn't be welcomed. No forgiving second chance would await us, no matter how much we long for reconciliation.

Rejection, abandonment, and shunning all trigger the pain center of the brain as powerfully as a slap across the face. The heartache is real: chest muscles contract. We hurt.

What choice do we have when our choices are taken from us?

My great-grandmother, Adoloratta Modello Bruno born in Caltanissetta, Sicily, had been a widow for years when she met a widower at Catholic mass; over time, they became close. She asked her son, my grandfather, for permission to marry. My grandfather told her if she remarried, she could "not cross his door or see her grandchildren again." She chose to marry the man she loved. My grandfather put a resounding end to the visits his wife and children paid to Nonna.

Being disowned: Have you heard of it? Some cultures, like my Sicilian one, have an "off with your head" dynamic: If you stray or do something that others disapprove of, you are no longer allowed in the family. My grandfather told my aunt Josephine she would "not cross his door again" if she smoked. When he found her cigarette pack, he disowned her.

For my great-grandmother and my aunt, there would be no second chance to rejoin their family.

This practice of disowning may sound like a relic from another century or another continent. But is it? Have you experienced or witnessed one person or

Comfort of
Little Things

Rejections hurt. Sometimes people want other people to suffer. Suffering is optional.

When a door is slammed in your face, ask yourself: How much of this stand-off is me and how much of it is the other person's?

Take responsibility for what is yours. Keep the focus on yourself and change what you can. Let go of trying to fix anyone else. Allow that person the dignity to make and learn from her own mistakes.

group shutting out another person or group with finality? Here are some modern-day disowning processes:

- A four-year-old girl on the playground puts her arm around another little girl and announces, "I'm not going to play with Madison for a hundred years. Are you?"
- A six-year-old child, born a boy, but who feels like a girl, is bullied by his classmates.
- An otherwise excellent teacher is terminated for making a mistake; no one else will hire her.
- A young black man, wearing a hoodie, is shot dead while walking home because he looks suspicious.

What choice do we have when our choices are taken from us?

I can try pretending that a wall hasn't been erected. I can try not acknowledging that I have experienced a loss. But denial only postpones the pain. When we are denied a second chance, we have to make our way through the darkness to find the light.

The steps I take to reclaim the light have become clear to me only in hindsight. Looking back, I realize that what I thought were dead ends became my greatest opportunities for growth. In no set order, below are the steps that help me.

- I grieve the loss. I grieve with sadness, anger, and sometimes (gallows) humor.
- I ask for help. I share my grief with people I trust.
- I choose to accept what is and let go of asking "What if . . . ?".
- I pray for serenity and a soothed heart.
- I pray to let go of resentment.
- I examine my part in the rupture and take responsibility for my wrongdoing.
- I do my best to make things right. If I cannot do this with the person who has closed the door, I pay it forward by doing acts of kindness and/or courage for others.
- I pray for the other person's well-being, regardless of how much I have been

hurt.

- I become grateful for the freedom that comes from accepting the things I cannot change and changing the things I can.

In the end, I give myself the second chance that the other person could not or did not give me (or herself). Even though my process takes years, I am heartened by my belief that things do get better. As author Henri Nouwen advised, we become the most spiritual in the places where we are the most broken.

When an important door has been closed on you or when you have been disowned by another person or group:

- How have you managed to deal with the loss?
- Who or what has helped you?
- What have you learned that might help others facing rejection?
- Did you find a way to give yourself, and others, a second chance?

When someone isn't willing to give us a second chance, there are steps we can take action inside ourselves to create our own second chances. Can we do anything with the person who locked us out? Should we bother to try? Usually conflicts are mutual, with both people sharing some responsibility. If I want to apologize and set things right for my part in the rupture, how can I do that? In these situations, I live by the following principle:

I do my best to make things right. If I cannot do this with the person who has closed the door, I pay it forward by bestowing acts of kindness and/or courage on others.

—Holly Elissa, June 18, 2014

When It Is Not Possible to Make Amends

A colleague never resolved his conflicts with his prior supervisor. The supervisor died, leaving a hole in my colleague's heart. Here's how my colleague made an amend. He paid it forward by becoming the most competent and compassionate and humble supervisor he could be.

Paying it forward by being of service to another person who is in some way similar to the person who shut you out is one way of making amends.

If you felt you were disrespectful to an older person at work, make a point of being of service to another senior. Taking the time to listen fully to that person may be all it takes. Sit with her. Hear her stories. Learn from her. Or she might need you to help her with a task that has become difficult now that she has aged. Help her.

As you do something to help this person who is similarly situated to the person with whom you have the conflict, you will know you have done something meaningful. Most likely, the person you have helped will view you as a gift from the heavens.

Spiritually, as we pay it forward, we hand out second chances like lollipops to anyone who passes us by. You know the saying: One door closes so another can open. Lyra might become an advocate for appropriate use of cell phones by teachers. Trixie Marie might tell everyone to whom she gossiped about Yalena, "I was wrong. Yalena has taught me a lot. She's a good supervisor." And you?

Making Amends to Yourself

Sometimes, the most difficult person with whom to make an amend is yourself. If I feel bad enough about what I have done or failed to do, I can deny myself comfort and understanding. Guess what? As I do little things to be of service to myself, I make an amend to others, including the person who locked me out. We are all always worthy of unconditional love and acceptance.

A Matter of Control and Powerlessness

A wise early childhood educator told me, "It's easier to blame ourselves for a problem and feel guilty about it than it is to accept that there's not a thing we can do to make things better." Feeling powerless is heart wrenching. We are helpers, nurturers, counselors, teachers, leaders. In all these roles, we have the power to make a difference. But what if we have no power? What if no one will listen to us? Simone de Beauvoir, author of *The Second Sex*, said a woman cannot be an authority unless other people accept her as an authority. How exhausting to feel competent and strong, yet have no one else believe you are capable of doing what you know you can do.

In truth, we are powerless over all people, places, and things. As one of my staff members warned me, "You can't push a rope." Trust me, I found the power within me to make sure this staff member did his job or moved on. In truth also, I could not change him. Only he could do that. However, I can set the standard for what behavior I will accept and what I will not accept. And I can enforce my standard by not allowing myself to be a doormat.

In cases where we have authority (as in this boss-employee situation), we have power to enforce the standards and to offer second chances. In places where we have no authority, we still have power. We can trust ourselves to create, offer, and accept a second chance, even when the door slams in our face, or the brick wall is too high and wide for us to overcome.

Reflection Questions

1. Have you had a door slammed in your face? When another person turned her back and cut you off from options, what have you been able to do? If you were able to come to peace with that situation, what helped you? If you are willing to do this, recall a time when you shut the door on another person. Would you do anything differently today?

2. In chapter 2, teacher Lyra shut the door on herself, refusing to do anything but blame herself. If you have observed or experienced a person who condemns herself without recourse to a second chance, what would you now recommend to do in that situation? Does timing matter? If so, how?

3. When two colleagues refuse to work with each other, saying they have an irreconcilable personality conflict, how do you feel? What do the children learn when adults slam doors on one another? Given that some relationships are unfixable, what steps can we take to model for children that adults can separate, move on, and learn from their irreconcilable differences?

4. How is a door being slammed in your face a spiritual opportunity for you? Where are the possible second chances in that seemingly one-sided equation?

Give Yourself a Break

Are you being loyal to someone else's harsh judgment of you? My "was-band" (he was my husband) told me I didn't have a solo voice (a.k.a. I shouldn't sing in our home). On my birthday this year, I woke up singing "Happy Birthday" to myself. Was I off-key? Don't know. Didn't care. Smiled the whole time.

What harsh judgment by another person is still holding you back? Take one small step at a time to prove that person wrong. You are capable, you are talented. You have strength. You have the right to define yourself.

5. In your experience, what is the difference between forgiveness and acceptance? Does being forgiven convey a different judgment from being accepted? Would you prefer to be accepted or forgiven? Both?

Chapter 10

When We Think We Can't, We Can

Only those who will risk going too far can possibly
find out how far one can go.—*T. S. Eliot*

Conflict is foreign to nurturers. We prefer to "love people through" conflict rather than confront the people. This soft approach isn't always the wiser choice. Sometimes "tough love," that seemingly in-your-face, calling-you-out directness is the truer path. Confrontation frightens the majority of educators.

Without conflict, we limit creativity. Without conflict resolution, we have hidden battles within secret wars. If we name things, we can deal with them. When we think we cannot do something, like resolve a conflict, that impasse is exactly the time to open ourselves to a second chance. If we name things, we can deal with them. If we name what separates us, we can begin to find our way to understanding.

Our old foe the Bully of Fear makes conflict even more difficult. An example of how fear can affect the decisions we make in our day-to-day lives was the news of the Ebola virus. With the steady stream of information we'd been exposed to about this deadly disease—some of it true, some of it not true—it's easy to understand why fear took us over for a while. Here's a reflection I posted in October 2014, when fear about Ebola was at its greatest:

Should I Go to Dallas? Would You?

Thousands of eager and spirited early childhood professionals convene annually for a friendly, often crowded, bustling, and eventful professional conference, sponsored by NAEYC. We fly in from around the country (and the world), riding shoulder to shoulder in trains, shuttles, taxis, and cars. For four days, we interact, hug, and sometimes sneeze, primarily in
public spaces.

In our field, we share. We share rooms, cabs, meals, and intimate conversations. We are literally a touching profession.

This year, beginning November 4, our annual conference is slated for the Dallas Convention Center. Lately, when you think of Dallas, does either the Dallas Cowboy football team or a soap opera about rich Texans come to mind?

Not likely. Instead we think of Thomas Eric Duncan, who died from the Ebola virus at Texas Health Presbyterian Hospital. We think of Mr. Duncan's two nurses, Nina Pham and Amber Vinson, who suffered from the Ebola virus for a few weeks after caring for Duncan. We can picture the deeply mourning countenance of Mr. Duncan's mother, Nowai Gartay, in Salisbury, North Carolina.

Newscasters tell us that an elementary school teacher in Maine, who attended another conference for educators (at a venue 9.5 miles from Mr. Duncan's hospital), has been placed on a 21-day leave due to "parents' concerns." Middle school students in Mississippi were pulled out of their classes because their principal had visited Zambia. Zambia is 3,000 miles away from the Ebola outbreak in Africa. As I wait for my car to be serviced in Auburn, Massachusetts, I ask an employee: "What's your take on the Ebola situation?" As soon as she finishes telling me how afraid she is, she decides to wipe down everything around her with disinfectant.

Should I go to Dallas for the NAEYC conference? Would you go?

NAEYC assures us that health precautions will be "heightened" to keep us safe.

Fight, flight, or freeze: These are our usual human responses to danger. We dig in our heels and crouch for a fight. We turn and sprint for the hills. Or we hold our breath and hope to fade into invisibility. When the bear lumbers out of the forest toward us or the guard dog snarls and growls, we seek safety.

More than anything, we want to survive and we want danger to go away. When threatened, we can't think clearly. Our system, under the command of the protective amygdala gland, throbs with adrenaline and cortisol. If we speak, we might say something we may later regret. If we make decisions, those decisions are not likely to be reasoned.

In short, we are rarely philosophical when we are terrified. Regaining perspective takes muscular effort. Because our core commitment in early childhood is "Do no harm," we devote ourselves to protecting children. Even if we don't fear for ourselves, we may question whether our being in Dallas will put the children in our care in danger.

Fear spreads faster than Ebola. When I mentioned that I flew through Dallas a few weeks ago, the person with whom I spoke backed away. Approximately 5 million people fly through Dallas each month. In fact, the entire population of Dallas would be quarantined if we all followed the standard used by that one Maine school system.

As with the Black Plague and the AIDS epidemic, fear touches everyone. Ask anyone around you about the "Ebola threat." No one has been untouched. The information available on the Internet has the ability to either fan those flames of fear, or extinguish them and put people at ease.

What we need more than anything else is accurate, useful data: Will going to Dallas put me in danger? What kind of danger? If I go to Dallas, will I in turn put anyone else in danger? What can I do to remain safe and virus-free if I travel to Dallas?

Consider these facts, which have been obscured by fear:

- Dozens of people in Dallas have completed the twenty-one-day quarantine. They are not infected.

- The World Health Organization declared that Nigeria is free of the Ebola virus. No new cases have been reported in more than forty days. Ebola can be contained.

- Theresa Romero (in Spain), the first person to develop Ebola outside of Africa (from missionaries who had been in Africa), has survived her bout with the illness.

- The health worker who quarantined herself aboard the "Ebola cruise" has tested negative for the virus.

Will I go to Dallas? Yes. Will I give my three presentations? Yes. Will I enjoy connecting with old friends and making new friends? Yes. Will we hug one another? Probably. Will I go out of my way to wash/sanitize my hands? Call me crazy, but I am likely to keep doing what I already do—use common sense, and use hand sanitizer before I eat a meal.

Would you go to Dallas? What facts would help you make that decision? If fear has ever controlled your life, how did you reclaim your peace of mind?

When we are overtaken by fear, we can't examine the facts and reflect on our options. Fear can both alert us and blind us.

At best, fear can offer us a second chance to research, to learn, and to make informed decisions. I am not fearful of contracting Ebola in Dallas. I intend to enjoy the conference and my colleagues. I do, however, fear for the children of Liberia and Sierra Leone who will continue to suffer until systems and resources can be put in place to protect them.

When we are driven by fear, we are owned by fear. When we are owned by fear, we cannot notice possibilities, or trust the future will get better. Fear chills the heart and flatlines the imagination. Worst of all, fear robs us of hope. Hope is what second chances are all about. By owning our fear before our fear owns us, we find the pathway to hope.

—Holly Elissa, October 21, 2014

Here's how one reader of my Dallas reflection focused on the threat of fear more than the threat of the illness:

Would You?

As a director here in Dallas, one who has had to navigate through the concerns of parents over Ebola, I've learned a few things. I reviewed our procedures for sanitization and safety. In the end, we realized that there wasn't any more than what we are already doing to maintain health and safety standards on a day to day basis. Even stating that health precautions will be heightened could be interpreted as our school not following precautions to the utmost to begin with. I realized that when a big event strikes, parents—who often create a large portion of their identity through the relationship and care of their children—seek the school out to ease their anxiety. They want to know their children are safe. If their children are safe, they feel safe. For the most part their children are, but I as the director am not able to give a full pledge that their child will never get hurt within our care. Random events that are out of our control do occur. There is always a potential for danger, however, it is events like Ebola [that] change our perception of that potential. The role of the director is to stay logical, to provide comfort if possible, but not to add to the frenzy. And we need to provide emotional support to directors as much as possible who can become the magnet for everyone else's anxiety.

—Cori Berg, October 22, 2014

Not everything that is faced can be changed, but nothing can be changed until it is faced.

—James Baldwin

Naming It

The first step in addressing fear is naming what we fear. As an educator, individual, and adult in the twenty-first century, what do you fear the most? What gives you the greatest hope? I'll go first.

As an educator, I fear children will be lost before we can reach them. More specifically, I fear they will be:

- lost to poverty;
- lost to their parent's addictions;
- lost on their way to America;
- lost to a screen that cannot hug them and;
- lost to the healing but disappearing world of fireflies and hopping toads.

As an individual, I fear:

- losing people I love, and;
- losing my capacity to be of use to others and myself; and
- confronting my deepest demons who threaten me with panic attacks and PTSD nightmares.

As an adult in the twenty-first century, I fear we won't outgrow our need for war quickly enough. And sure, I also fear:

- heights (if I have to look straight down);
- spiders (if they are climbing on my skin);
- root canals; and
- confronting headstrong people.

The next question, then, is about hope. What is it that gives you the greatest hope? I have boundless hope. I have witnessed miracles both tiny and rhapsodic:

* downhearted people who find happiness
* cruelty edged out by kindness
* children who appeared to have grave difficulties triumph because someone loves them

Now it's your turn: What are your greatest fears, and what gives you hope? As educators, if we picture the face of a curious child, how can we not have hope?

The Source of All Fear, according to Freud

Our fears, however, can edge out hope. To go to the core of why fear dominates us, we might need to look to psychoanalyst Sigmund Freud. Freud claims that all of our fears stem from one great fear: our fear of dying.

Does Freud's concept make sense to you? It does to me. We fear what is unseen more than what is seen. We fear what we cannot control. We fear coming face-to-face with astounding power. We fear both what that power might do and how we might respond or fail to respond. We run from a fate we all inevitably face.

We die. So far, that's inevitable.

We must use time wisely and forever realize that the time is always ripe to do right.
—Nelson Mandela

Surrendering to the unknown on the other side of death requires trust. Trust to risk opening our heart. Faith to risk letting go of all that we know. Now there's a challenge. Where's the second chance in that?

Of course, things that appear to be inevitable are not always so. Stunning and unimagined inventions and creations have been known to wipe out what we thought was a given. I was born on the last day of 1945, the year in which World War II ended.

I was born before polio had a cure, before birth control pills were invented, before the Internet buzzed with connectivity, before the Berlin Wall was cracked by wrecking balls, before Nelson Mandela created the reconciliation process, and before Americans elected a black man as president. Maya Angelou had not yet revealed why the caged bird sings. Neil Armstrong had not yet taken one giant leap for humanity. Lucy was not in the sky with diamonds. Marvin Gaye hadn't heard it through the grapevine.

I met a man who plans to have his body frozen when he dies. He is leaving directives and a trust so he can be thawed when science has progressed to a place where all illnesses can be healed. He believes death will be outwitted eventually. He wants to be around when that happens. Could what he believes be true?

Freud's statement can make us question assumptions. How about we question our assumption that confrontation is evil and mean-spirited? How about we question our assumption that we might not survive those wretched feelings that lead to a face-to-face confrontation? How about we challenge ourselves to face what we fear most, one step at a time?

Educators' Fear of Conflict and Confrontation

As educators, most of us don't like conflict. Confrontation is our four-letter word. We are peacemakers and supporters, nurturers and builders. Not only do we not like fighting, we fear fighting. Most of us do, anyway.

Now let's look at a compelling principle of second chances: Our greatest opportunities await us in the most difficult places. In the everyday difficult places. Where families split up and teachers lose their jobs. Where children are bullied and adults exclude others. Where battles rage above ground and fester beneath the surface.

In these, the most feared of everyday places, we find the greatest liberation and the greatest hope. However, to get to hope, we have to step up to the challenge. We need to name and practice the step-by-step process to claim the courage and stamina within to stick with it through the scariest parts. Following is one small example of a second chance in the midst of potential disconnection.

Comfort in Little Things

Name one thing that has come to pass that you never thought would happen. It just didn't seem possible that something so entrenched would change; but amazingly, it happened.

Now think of one thing that gives you hope for the future. What helps you believe that things are getting better, despite the preponderance of bad news?

Keep your eyes on that prize: Mountains do move. The glass is half-full. You are part of the change for the better.

Standing Up to Unworthiness: When a Child Calls a Mother Out

I love my son, Nick, forever and always. Nick knows he is loved. Feeling lovable is necessary, especially during upheavals.

Moving into a new place is disruptive for anyone. Boxes have to be packed and unpacked. Utilities disconnected and installed. Mail, rerouted. Habits that make life easier, like knowing the pathway to the bathroom in the dark, have to be newly created. New neighbors present universes to be learned. Grocery store aisles are unfamiliar. You know the drill.

For Nick, moving is doubly challenging. Nick is disabled. His disabilities are not visible to the eye. Nick struggles openly with anger management.

When Nick is uneasy, he transfers his discomfort to another person. Mom is a likely suspect. After all, no matter how raggedy or all-elbows a child gets, he knows Mom will love him through it.

One week after his move, Nick and I had lunch at a Thai restaurant. Nothing on the menu pleased him. That same night, with family friends, Nick loudly raged: "Mom! You didn't do this. Mom, remember you didn't do that! Mom! Mom!" I called on my usual tools for oppositional defiant disorder: breathe, listen, don't get hooked, state and maintain my boundaries. By the end of the evening, however, my buttons had been pushed.

I don't like the raw feelings (resentment, hurt, rage) that can spew like a geyser during conflicts. But I knew Nick and I needed to talk. Avoiding that conversation the next morning would have been easy. The storm would pass, but the monsoon would continue to threaten.

So I said to my son of thirty years: "I love you. I get that you are angry with me. I apologize for the things I didn't get right as your mom. Let's get help from a counselor if you feel that would help." To which Nick said, "Mom, I'm sorry I said mean things to you."

That's all it took. We began to talk again and haven't stopped since. Pretending the day of rage hadn't happened was an option. Denial, however, wipes out second chances. As in most conflicts of the heart, humility is the balm of Gilead. Mother and child reunions require humility. Nick and I have a lifetime of second chances ahead of us. My hunch? We will need them, and we will take them.

When you give yourself a second chance to ease a conflict in your family and/or your work family, consider the following questions:

* How easy or difficult is it to step back from the heat of the conflict?
* When someone has hurt your feelings, are you likely to offer a second chance?
* What do you do if a person refuses to take or give a second chance, or dies before a second chance is possible?

—Holly Elissa, July 15, 2014

When I discuessed this topic on the blog, reader Jo-Ann Spence made the following reply:

Standing Up to Unworthiness: When a Child Calls a Mother Out

My mom and I spent forty-five minutes on the phone talking about people we were worrying about among other things. After talking about all we have tried to do about a bad situation a family member is in and what will happen if the situation continues, I said, "Wouldn't it be nice if people would live their lives the way we think they should? We'd certainly pick out a happier life for them." We laughed, and now when we find ourselves endlessly worrying about this person or that person, we say, "Well, if they would live their lives the way we think they should!" It helps us laugh a little when we feel so full of love and worry and know we have tried to help and we can't. It is a strange thing about life that those who need help seem powerless to take it or powerless over their own feelings. Those of us on the outside can get carried away by the flood of someone else's neediness. My mom and I have often had sleepless nights trying to think what we can do when the truth is we can't fix anyone! But we can love them, and lend an ear or a ride or whatever is in our power to share. And we can love each other and reach out to each other when the tide is trying to wash us away with it. We can let our happy lives be an example for others.

—Jo-Ann Spence, August 28, 2014

The truth of life is only revealed through exchanges between many individuals.
—François Cheng

My response:

Dear Jo,

Thank you for the reminder that much of this powerlessness principle is counterintuitive. When we love, we want to help, to stop the pain, to make things softer and easier. That drive, especially for moms (and probably dads too), is intense. We hugged and soothed and comforted our kids when they were little. When they are adults, we pray they can take care of themselves. When they don't (or don't in the way we want them to), oh my, that's painful: "It's a strange thing in life that those who need help seem powerless to take it or powerless over their own feelings." Here's what helps me let go: we all need to face those devils running around in our hearts ourselves. There's no getting away from that. Other people can love us through wrenching times; but other people can't do the walking for us. Those sleepless nights? They happen when I try to change another person. Honey, as I said, I have enough work making (and deciding to make) the changes I need to make to be free. In the end, I choose to believe that loving unconditionally is my truest path, especially when I remember I am worthy of that love too!

Be always kind to you,

—Holly Elissa

Dirty Words: *Conflict, Confrontation*

Does anyone relish conflict? Perhaps a bungee jumper who dives off the bridge counterintuitively toward the rocky river below. Perhaps people who are into other extreme sports and have a high tolerance for adrenaline rushes. Perhaps the tightrope walker who balances over Niagara Falls. Perhaps the bully who wields power through threats and intimidation. Perhaps athletes who compete to defeat a rival team. Or maybe lawyers who believe arguing is the way to knock truth out of conflicting statements about what actually happened.

Perhaps these people have a "long fuse" or a high tolerance for dread and danger. Perhaps their systems crave the adrenaline rush. Perhaps they are on one end of the continuum, and most educators are on the other.

Does the amygdala like conflict? Who knows? What we do know is that the amygdala sweeps the fields around us for signs of conflict. When conflict crops up, or threatens to crop up, the amygdala commands us to fight back or run for the safety of the hills. The amygdala does its job: it keeps us safe.

If you hear a voice inside you say, "You cannot paint," then by all means paint, and that voice will be silenced.

—Vincent van Gogh

The amygdala does not, however, help us understand or gain perspective or be spiritually free. Only in partnership with the prefrontal cortex, like when a messenger hands off a top-secret message to a general, can the amygdala help us be deeply free. When we are free, we can notice where we are. We can see our second chance patiently awaiting us. When we are free to choose, we can choose a second chance.

Conflict can be a stimulus for survival or for renewal. Choosing renewal takes courage.

What's the Story with Educators and Our Dance with Conflict?

Do educators enjoy conflict and confrontation? Let's start with you. Ask yourself how comfortable you are with conflict, especially with confronting another person. Where would you locate yourself on a scale of 1 to 10, using the following key?

1 = strongly dislike;

2 = prefer to avoid;

3, 4, 5, 6 = can do but don't like;

7, 8, 9 = prefer to address;

10 = welcome conflict/skilled confronter.

Most education leaders tell me they fall into the 5 to 7 categories; teachers place themselves in the 1 to 4 categories. Those who gave themselves a higher rating explain quickly: "It's not that I like conflict. It's just that I know I have to deal with it." Educators who say they are in the 1 to 4 categories explain that they hate confrontation and would rather avoid it and just take a positive approach to everyone and everything. "I can't take confrontation," teachers tell me. "I'd rather teach children than deal with adults."

Our research at Wheelock College revealed that fully 80 percent of early childhood leaders are conflict-avoidant, prefer harmony, and have a strong dislike or fear of confrontation (Bruno and Copeland 2012, 123). Other research tells us that 70 percent of women and 44 percent of men take things personally, are "sensitive" to having their feelings hurt, and shy away from conflict (Myers et al. 1998). Perhaps because our leaders were (and many still wish they could be) teachers first, if given the option, these leaders would rather gently support than forcibly confront.

These percentages are not surprising, are they? Our mission as educators is to help people learn and grow. Our practice is to be supportive, caring, and gentle. Conflict is not gentle. We prefer "reflective supervision" to the more confrontational "directive supervision" (Bruno 2012). We prefer to help people discover their strengths rather than to "bang them over the head" with their shortcomings. Our literature maintains that children learn best when they feel safe, loved, culturally respected, and accepted for who they are. Why should we think adults are any different than children?

Looking back on the effect of our amygdala gland, we can see why conflict and confrontation are offensive to us. The result is avoidance. We avoid conflict. We walk what feels like the "higher" path, above the fray. Walk into any early childhood program and ask about the "unwritten" rules by which the center operates. You'll discover that "being nice" is a pervasive rule.

Consequences of Avoiding Conflict

There's nothing wrong with being nice. There's everything right about being respectful and loving and kind. There's also (surprisingly to some of us) everything right about conflict. When two human beings connect, we have differences. We need to negotiate the differences. Burying differences is a certain pathway to disconnecting from one another.

This is what things can teach us: to fall, patiently to trust our heaviness. Even a bird has to do that before he can fly. —Rainer Maria Rilke, *Book of Hours: Love Letters to God*

You may be objective and analytical; I may be aware of and sensitive to people's feelings and unspoken desires. I need you to appreciate my capacity for emotional intelligence; you need me to appreciate your capacity for logic and hard reasoning. If we pretend we aren't different, our different styles will chew us up.

If we avoid talking out our differences, we will make judgments about one another. Soon enough, we will believe our judgments: You are heartless; I am a bleeding heart. The space between us becomes a minefield. We tip-toe around each other. Our workspace becomes toxic. We lose our energy to pretending. We begin to dislike our work. We begin to feel that we might burn out. Ugh. What are we modeling for children? What are we doing to our joie de vivre? A partnership that was once light, airy, and full of promise slides into a morass of dark, stifled heaviness.

Choosing Freedom or Choosing the Status Quo

Have you been in this situation? Experienced this dynamic? Take a look at what you chose to do. Knowing that answer is instrumental to your understanding of what you need to do to be free. And of what you need to do to show children that differences are like breathing: we go in and out of them regularly. Take a look also at when you have felt wholeheartedly free, happy with yourself and your life.

My hunch: You catapulted yourself into freedom by facing something that was difficult for you. You didn't run away from it (or if you did, you turned around and walked back). You took a stand. You took action. You did what you knew was the right thing. You made a hard decision.

Once you made that decision, you stepped into the light and were knighted on both shoulders by the sword of dignity and hope. You stepped out of your confusion and darkness into the second chance that was always waiting for you. Your pathway was not only cleared, it became clearer to you. You got another clue about what you are on Earth to be and do.

The opposite of being nice isn't being mean. The opposite of being nice is being authentic. Covering up a difference helps no one in the long run. In the short run, by covering up a conflict, we feel temporarily okay, if not safe.

In the depth of winter, I finally learned that within me there lay an invincible summer.
—Albert Camus

Together our amygdala and prefrontal cortex will haunt us like the hounds of heaven if we don't face up to conflict. Avoiding conflict is a slippery slope to despair. First, we will feel a little off-kilter. Second, little things get under our skin. Third, those little things start to push our buttons. Fourth, we try to run away and pretend everything is fine. Then, our spirit takes a slow and steady, or even precipitous slide. We start seeing the world as a darker, less safe and hospitable place. We become resentful. We lose our power. In so doing, we lose who we are. We lose our strength, self-respect, and passion for making a difference.

But I still hate conflict, you might say. *I'd rather put up with what I've got than stir things up.* You will always have that choice. Sometimes, living with what you've got will be the better choice. It's always the easier choice. After a while, though, you may ask yourself: Do I want to live or to exist? When just getting through the day without a scuffle no longer suffices, you may make another choice. When work becomes alien and joyless, happiness at home becomes less likely. So, here it is: Will I choose to live my life or get through my life?

Choosing to Live My Life: Steps to Saying "Yes" to a Second Chance

When it comes to choosing to live our lives fully and deeply, there is much agreement: Just do it. Here are the steps:

1. Name what's pushing your buttons: What are the behaviors? Words?

2. Identify patterns that are emerging: Are you overlaying any past conflict on this situation? Are you taking a stand or avoiding the conflict?

3. Practice defusing your amygdala, preventing it from hijacking your integrity: use the tools we learned in chapter 4, from breathing to praying.

4. Ask for and accept help.

5. Take responsibility for changing what you need to change; let go of trying to change anyone else.

6. Ask yourself, "Do I want to be free, or do I want to get by? Is avoiding the scary feelings that come with confrontation more important than stepping up to confront?"

7. Establish your support system: Whom can you text, call, or get a hug from? Choose only trustworthy and loving people.

8. Decide what you want out of this confrontation: How do you want to act and feel as a result? Acknowledge, then dismiss any desire to "make the other person change."

9. Practice the confrontation until you feel as ready as you can be.

10. Relax your ego: Step aside from any need to control the outcome, be victorious, or feel morally superior. This confrontation is about freedom, not enslavement. Go into the confrontation with humility.

11. Arrange the confrontation. Set it up to be in an environment where you feel safe and strong and can breathe.

12. Sit beside the other person (rather than across from her).

13. Say what the issue is that divides you without blaming or shaming the other person. Hold up the issue as a challenge to resolve together.

14. Say what you will do to set things right.

15. Invite the other person to name the issue between you (if the person blames or shames you, use your tools for calling on your executive function).

16. Take a break as needed.

17. Listen to what the other person proposes as the solution, or to whether she thinks a solution is possible. Come to a decision that harms no one and uplifts everyone and is in service to your greater purpose.

18. Take time to "sleep on it" if either of you needs that time.

19. Notice where you are: What is the second chance patiently waiting for both of you or for you as a result of facing your fears?

Each time you walk these steps, you will find the process gets easier. You will grow in confidence. Your fear will subside. Your fears will lessen. You will trust yourself more. You will feel more mature. You will feel less at the mercy of unkind forces. You will find other second chances waiting over and over and over again. In the end, you will likely decide, as I have, that life is more beautiful than you ever imagined and that everyone's suffering can be eased or even healed. You will inspire others. You will be full of gratitude.

Applying the Steps to the Case Study of Nick and Me

Let's put these steps to work. I invite you to consider how you might use these steps in your own unresolved conflict. First, here's how Nick and I used the steps:

1. Name what's pushing your buttons: What are the behaviors? Words? *Hearing negative judgments about myself without a letup.*

2. Identify patterns that are emerging: Are you overlaying any past conflict on this situation? Are you taking a stand or avoiding the conflict? *Yes, my father was negative to me without letup. His actions depressed me. I need to remind myself that Nick is my son, not my father.*

3. Practice defusing your amygdala, preventing it from hijacking your integrity: Use the tools we learned in chapter 4, from breathing to praying. *I breathe. I listen. I remind myself not to get hooked. I tell Nick he needs to stop. I step away.*

4. Ask for and accept the help you need. *I pray for help. Meanwhile, my friend Karen stays with Nick, reminding him to "deal with it."*

5. Take responsibility for changing what you need to change; let go of trying to change anyone else. *I accept I made mistakes as Nick's mom. I am willing to get help to talk this through and to make changes.*

6. Ask yourself, "Do I want to be free, or do I want to get by? Is avoiding the scary feelings that come with confrontation more important than stepping up to confront?" *I want to be free. I hate feeling despondent and beaten down.*

Give Yourself a Break

You have taken a stand for what matters to you. You have taken this stand regardless of opposition.

Recall a stand that you have taken. What did you stand for? Who opposed you? What helped you keep your dedication and your conviction?

Remember, you have fought for what matters. You did it before. You will do it again. Each time, you learn more and get better at the process. Give yourself credit, peacemaker!

7. Set up your support system: Who can you text, call, or get a hug from? Choose only trustworthy and loving people. *I go to church and pray for help. I pray for Nick and for both of us.*

8. Decide what you want out of this confrontation: How do you want to act and feel as a result? Acknowledge, then dismiss any desire to "make the other person change." *I want us to work through our differences. I want us to find a process that works for us both. I want to tell Nick I love him and that I believe we can do this.*

9. Practice the confrontation until you feel as ready as you can be. *Okay, I skipped this one; however, I did think through what I wanted to say.*

10. Relax your ego: Step aside from any need to control the outcome, be victorious, or feel morally superior. This confrontation is about freedom, not enslavement. Go into the confrontation with humility. *Prayer almost always gives me humility. I am ready to be vulnerable and not defensive.*

11. Arrange the confrontation. Set it up to be in an environment where you feel safe and strong and can breathe. *I wait until Nick and I are sitting beside one another in the car. We have both had a good night's sleep. We can stop the car any time we need to take a break. We have done this before.*

12. Sit beside the other person (rather than across from her). *Done. This works much better for us. Being face-to-face sometimes leads to being defensive, not collaborative.*

13. Say what the issue is that divides you without blaming or shaming the other person. Hold up the issue as a challenge for you both to resolve together. *Nick, I love you. I hear that you are unhappy with things I did and failed to do as your mom.*

14. Say what you will do to set things right. *I am willing to see a counselor with you. Do you think that will help?*

15. Invite the other person to name the issue between you (if the person blames or shames you, use your tools for calling upon your executive function). *Nick says: "Mom, I'm sorry I said mean things to you. We got help before from counseling. I think we are okay."*

16. Take a break as needed.

17. Listen to what the other person proposes as the solution, or to whether she thinks a solution is possible. Come to a decision that harms no one

and uplifts everyone and is in service to your greater purpose. *Nick says: "Mom we're good." I feel we are too. We are talking. We have made amends. We have set a precedent for the next time.*

18. Take time to "sleep on it" if either of you needs that time. *Done. We both needed time away from the difficult day we had shared.*

19. Notice where you are: What is the second chance patiently waiting for both of you or for you as a result of facing your fear? *I feel relieved. Nick is looser too. We are able to laugh and joke and talk freely on the way home. I realize how much I love my son and how proud I am of each of us for having come as far as we have together. I feel grateful and free.*

Whew! That took a lot of energy. I can tell you though, courage was worth it. I don't do well when I am yelled at, especially by a male who is larger than I am. I faced that fear. My humility may have allowed, or at least invited, Nick to put aside his rage.

What If I Don't Get the Steps Right? Or I Don't Get through Them?

I have taken the same steps in work situations as I did in the conflict with my son. In the beginning, facing my fear of confrontation was almost impossible. I got foot cramps, felt inadequate, worried and worried, and avoided until I couldn't stand the feeling anymore. I got "sick and tired of being sick and tired." Each time, I held my own and kept the focus on myself. I let go of my need to change the other person.

Did I fail? Sure. Some people have been so irate with me that resolution wasn't possible. They felt I was totally in the wrong. Or they thought I was an inadequate person. In these cases, where talking things through wasn't possible, I made amends to the extent I was able. I made amends to the person directly when that was possible, taking responsibility for my part in the conflict. If I was blocked from making an amend to the person directly, I practiced my new behavior in another setting with a determination to change the things I can for the better.

Did I beat myself up at times? Sure. It's hard to be judged inadequate and fully wrong. It's painful to want to make things better and to be shut out of that possibility. At times, being hard on myself was easier than admitting I was powerless over the situation. Today, I am more able to accept that I am powerless over others.

Comfort in Little Things

Humor is a saving grace. When we laugh at our own foibles, we lighten up on ourselves. In so doing we ease the tension of the folks around us.

When have you used humor or poked fun at yourself to help diffuse a mean-spirited conflict?

Give yourself credit for being able to laugh, especially at yourself. In fact, right now, what can you find laughable about yourself?

The page isn't long enough for me to list those things.

The only way to discover the limits of the possible is to go beyond them into the impossible.

—Arthur C. Clarke

I am glad to say I no longer need to make the other person into a bad guy. I have come to see that some situations are not going to be remedied with this person in this lifetime. The questions to ask are, What can I learn? How can I be more mature with the next person? How can I share what I am learning to uplift my community, to bring hope to everyone I meet?

Reflection Questions

1. If you were to apply this chapter's conflict-resolution steps right now to an unresolved conflict, describe how you would implement each step to make it your own.

2. What do you fear most? Have you had moments in your life when you were able to face that fear? What resources (inner and external) can you call on to help you feel the fear but not be paralyzed by it?

3. What helps you focus on yourself and what you can do, rather than getting hooked by the other person's accusations and/or making that person out to be the "bad guy"?

4. What process would you use with children, if you have a conflict with a child? How might you modify the steps in this chapter to be age appropriate?

5. If someone at work decides you are inadequate and is not willing to talk things out with you, what options do you have? Can you find ways to work successfully in the same organization as that person? Or is the negativity too toxic to reach a resolution?

Part IV   Creating a Culture of
Second Chances

 Offering Second Chances to Others

"Paying It Forward" without Demanding Payback

Real generosity is doing something nice for someone
who will never find out.—*Frank A. Clark*

One challenge at a time, throughout this book, we have named, pondered, and—I hope—addressed what hinders or helps us open our hearts to receive second chances. I have been working from my underlying assumption: We educators tend to be far more generous offering second chances to others than we are to noticing, asking for, or accepting second chances for ourselves. Being both able and willing to accept second chances when offered and to create or request second chances when they are not offered is the platform for a joyously fulfilling life. As Thich Nhat Hanh said, "The most important thing is for each of us to have some freedom in our heart, some stability in our heart, and some peace in our heart. Only then will we be able to relieve the suffering around us."

Building on our strengths and hope, we can now interact with others in order to create a culture of second chances. Each moment is as much an opportunity for awe as it is an opportunity for growth. We need both.

As educators, we know that our every action is a lesson to children. Let that lesson be compassion toward ourselves and others.

What If We All Wanted to Come to Work?

How would your workplace look if colleagues were open to the magic of second chances?

Imagine your workplace popping to life with delightful surprises: coworkers offering acts of loving and creative kindness to one another, to children, to families, and to anyone else who walks through the door. These acts can be random acts, selectively intentional acts, or both. You can target a specific person or team, or you can throw kindness to the wind and notice where the seeds fall.

Imagine colleagues doing kind things for one another anonymously without expecting payback. Imagine coworkers giving freely without that controlling quid-pro-quo, you-owe-me-one mentality. Imagine finding your favorite flower in a small vase in your workspace or a coffee just the way you like it waiting for you when you enter the building. Imagine knowing that people care.

Could you stand it? Would you trust it? Can you do it?

What would it take for you to initiate or work with a team to create a culture of second chances? Making a difference like this by ourselves is fun, but making a difference with allies is heartening. Just doing it: that's the reward. And in these days of fiscal integrity, how cost-effective!

What a Culture of Second Chances Looks Like

You know you have created a culture of second chances when colleagues

- can't wait to get to work every day;
- don't foresee what awaits them, but believe something good is in store;
- catch on to the value in the comfort of little things and the magic in little moments;
- step back before judging one another negatively; in fact, look to find something of value in one another;
- pay it forward without expecting payback;
- willingly offer themselves and others the opportunity to make and learn from mistakes;
- laugh together, lighten up on themselves, and keep perspective on those human messes we get ourselves into;

- feel optimistic, knowing they are making a difference;
- feel secure and supported enough to grow and change; and
- model for children that adulthood is a good thing, full of learning, full of healing, full of opportunities, perhaps even full of understanding.

Definition of a "Culture of Second Chances"

A culture of second chances is a shared community ethic and practice where we help one another rather than diminish one another. We find ways to work through things, including our conflicts. We aim to find meaning in the everyday, and our hope kicks negativity to the curb. We have the power to create a culture of second chances. To create such a community, we need to continuously make choices for the greater good. A culture of second chances isn't just about me.

Sure, we feel more affinity for and comfort with some colleagues than others. That's natural. As we see others in a new light as a result of our paying it forward to them, we give ourselves a second chance: Be open to folk we had stereotyped or otherwise judged too quickly. In this way, the culture of second chances pays it forward to us as well.

The film *Pay It Forward*, released in 2000, gave us a new name for altruism, a phenomenon we have always known.

- **Altruism is humble compassion**, being of service, and comforting others (and ourselves) in little ways. With no price tag attached.
- **Paying it forward is giving freely, anonymously, and devoid of expectation.** The giving is everything. The person who gives knows what she gives, but no one else has to know the identity of the generous benefactor.

Paying it forward is what educators are all about. That's our secret to meaningful work. The world is a better place because we help one child, one moment at a time. Those moments add up to a lifetime of making a difference that doesn't quit.

Paying it forward requires letting go of manipulation, self-aggrandizement, and pettiness. We can't always meet this standard. However, the shared desire to do so helps us keep going when we stumble.

A Cause for Humility

A curious thing happens within me when I pay it forward. I get all happy when I offer something of value freely and anonymously. I prefer to disappear before I am discovered. I fear that I'll get caught in the act! I don't want the recipient to know who gave her the gift. I want to offer something of value without needing to hear "thank you." My desire is to be one among many in a world of kindhearted people.

I like to see people looking around them, wondering, *who was that kind, anonymous person?* Could it be you? Or him? What about that person over there? I like feeling that anyone can find kindheartedness in herself and share it with others. I like the softness in people's eyes when they sense kindheartedness in and around them.

Humility is finding that honest place of joy in ourselves and offering it to others without expectation. What the other person does or doesn't do with her gift isn't the point. The point is, kindness has been offered. Kindness has been extended into the world. In some pay-it-forward unseen way, the world sighs with appreciation. In truth, I don't always have this humility; however, I love it when I do.

Strings Attached? Time to Detach

Selflessly paying it forward is not always what we do. Have you, like I have, held the door for someone who does not acknowledge you?

That person walks through the door oblivious to me, full of entitlement, not noticing my kindness. That person's ungracious attitude kicks up dust bunnies of resentment: Hey! Just because I opened the door for you does not make me your servant!

At times, when a person fails to thank me, I righteously pronounce, "You're welcome." The snarkiness in my voice and demeanor indicates that the "thoughtless" person is anything but welcome. My message is: You're welcome. Not! Buzz off, you ungrateful jerk!

When I slide into this behavior, I'm not paying it forward. I'm looking for gratitude and affirmation. I expect to be acknowledged and recognized for my good deed. The recipient "owes" me. The least the recipient can do is say, "Thank you." Altruism falls prey to "it's all about me." I'm needy and "looking for love in all the wrong places." True altruism is detaching with love.

One Step at a Time to Pay It Forward

To pay kindness forward, we need some practical steps and savvy tips. Are you ready? Let's do this together, beginning with the vision of a fulfilling, uplifting, engagingly positive, and continuously creative community. Ready to walk the steps with me? Here are steps to creating a culture of second chances:

1. Prepare yourself.

   - Melt your ego. Ask yourself, can you pay it forward anonymously, or do you need recognition from others?
   - Set and honor boundaries. How much time and energy do you want to dedicate to the process?
   - Know what you can and cannot do. Remember, little things make a big difference.
   - Aim to be pure of heart. Check your intentions for any desire to manipulate.
   - Kiss good-bye the expectation of having control over anyone but yourself.
   - Pay attention. Take notice of what colleagues need and would love. Trust your intuitive heart to know while continuing to hone your knowledge.
   - Make a plan for when and how to take action.
   - Decide whether you want others to join you in paying it forward (see number 2 below).
   - Decide what you will say if you are asked if you were the one who gave the gift. You can say anything from "I promised I wouldn't reveal who did this" to "Yep, I'm the one." But remember, "outing" yourself limits your ability to pay it forward in the future.

Give Yourself a Break

Recall just one time when you did something for another person. Did your feeling of making a difference depend upon that person's thank you? Did the act of kindness itself affect the way you felt about yourself?

We aren't always selfless. Sometimes we need affirmation; we need praise. That's human too.

Now recall a time when someone did a kind thing for you, without your asking. What difference did that person and that act make to you?

2. Identify and enlist appropriate colleagues.

- Be on the lookout for like-hearted colleagues who are compassionate, mature, playful, resourceful, and responsible; know what you are looking for.
- Take time to get to know each potential ally, both inside and outside of the workplace.
- Ask the colleague: What are one or two things we could do anonymously to uplift and delight our coworkers? Would you like to join me in a "paying-it-forward" effort to make these things happen?
- Listen carefully to what you hear. Are the ideas respectful, new, appropriate, and likely to have the desired effect? What is your colleague's intention? If you are not clear on any of these, talk about your questions and concerns. You can always decide not to go forward.
- Determine who else needs to be included in the planning, or at least made aware of your plans. Make sure that you have management's endorsement.
- Think through the things that might go awry; have a plan for how to handle each challenge.
- Agree to an action plan.
- Document what you are doing and the permission(s) you have received.
- Enjoy the anonymity together.

3. Take action.

- Make sure the timing and setting are aligned to ensure your anonymity.
- Deliver the gift.
- Enjoy the magic of paying it forward (enjoy the feelings of doing something kind and unexpected).
- Congratulate yourself; let go of needing praise from others.
- Notice where you are when you see or hear that the gift has been discovered.
- Allow the light of that response to intensify the beacon in your heart.

Let's put these steps into effect in a typical work situation. As you read Ms. L'amora's case below, ask yourself: If L'amora asked for my advice, what would I say?

Lead infant teacher Ms. L'amora is concerned about her colleagues' exhaustion. Preparing for NAEYC accreditation was a long and demanding process with little financial reward. Everyone was on board and agreed going for accreditation was the right thing to do; however, few people realized how burned out they would feel not just from completing their classroom portfolios but also from the examiners' visit.

Even the director, Ms. Margo, has dark circles under her eyes and little energy remaining. Everyone knows Margo takes on too much responsibility; however, they also know Margo loves her work and her staff. Families, led by Mr. Ramos, head of the Family Advisory Team, are appreciative and would like to find a way to thank everyone at the center, including the custodian Ms. Agnes, the teachers' aides, the floaters, and, of course, Mr. Ronald, who is on paternity leave after the birth of his son, Ronald Jr. Mrs. Lartner, chair of the board, a busy disabilities attorney, doesn't have time to plan a celebration. However, she has told Mr. Ramos that there is funding for some kind of celebration.

While soothing one of the babies in her classroom and feeling pride in the center's accomplishment (regardless of what the accreditation outcome might be), Ms. L'amora decides she wants to thank everyone for their hard work. L'amora doesn't want anyone to know that the surprise she comes up with is her plan. She just wants to "give back" to her hardworking team anonymously.

Comfort in Little Things

Choose one way you will pay it forward anonymously in any one or all of these settings: at work, at the supermarket, at a family gathering. Now, add yourself to the list of recipients. Pay it forward to yourself. Ask yourself: if I were acting with love to myself right now, what would I do? Do it. And again. And again.

If L'amora asked for your advice, what would you say? Which of the steps could L'amora take?

Self-Care as Prerequisite to Paying It Forward

Paying it forward is offering a second chance without needing or expecting anything in return. When my cup is full, I pour over easily. When my cup is empty, I may use what appears to be an act of kindness to get even with an ungrateful world. As a victim, my only power is to bring other people down to my level. Victims become invested in being victims. A second chance would challenge a victim's identity.

We all qualify as victims. People hurt us. We define ourselves as having been wronged. Making things right is not a victim's instinct. Passing on pain is.

To create a culture of second chances with my colleagues, I need to attend to my own well-being first. When I am grateful and content, I am happy to do random acts of kindness. When I am hurting, I may not be ready to act selflessly. I have to first soothe and next outgrow the victim in me.

Paying it forward requires the maturity to give and let go. The act of giving is the reward. The act of giving itself pays back my heart many times over. Paying it forward means I detach from the outcomes. I offer a gift and let go. The giving is enough.

What Power Do We Have to Make a Difference to Colleagues?

The only person I can change is myself. However, as I change, those around me adjust. They choose how they adjust. I can offer something of value. They can choose to accept, reject, or ignore my offer. They make a choice. And in that choice making, they have more options than they had before.

Say, for example, that I decide I will not gossip and no one around me can pull me down into the negativity of gossiping. Some people will peddle their negativity elsewhere. Fine by me. Some people will shun me or leave me out of the gossip mill. Fine by me. Other people will enjoy talking about more productive things. Truly fine by me. I can't sabotage my second chance by allowing myself to be a people pleaser, selling out my own value in the hope of acceptance. This chapter focuses on what we can do, rather than frittering away our energies by looking only at what we cannot do.

What If Paying It Forward Doesn't Work?

When paying-it-forward efforts fail, they fail largely for the following reasons:

- You do not check in with the "proper authorities." For example, either Director Margo needs to be apprised or the board chair and parent advisory chair need to be given a heads-up.
- You expect to be praised for your "selfless" act. Go through the questions earlier in this chapter, including, Ask yourself, "Can I pay it forward anonymously, or do I need recognition from others?
- You expect to be acknowledged as the savior of the team.
- You do not know what the group would really like and make assumptions that should have been tested in advance.

If you are in doubt about what the group or individual needs, you can invite a trusted colleague to help you or find ways to talk with colleagues about what they may want. Ask questions like, "What would help you relax during your breaks from work?" or "If we were to do something together as a team, what would be the most fun for you?"

Honestly, if you have prepared yourself by taking the steps to call on your executive function and not get hooked negatively by your amygdala, you will stand a very good chance of knowing just how to plan the best possible way to pay it forward. Are you ready?

Each of these snafus can be addressed by reviewing the tips in the section "One Step at a Time to Pay It Forward" on page 145.

When paying it forward doesn't work, the issue is often in ourselves: We may be needy and not know it, expect to be rewarded and not see it, or want to boost our sagging confidence by doing good. Paying it forward or offering second chances requires that we get clear on our intention. Step back if what appears to be an act of compassion is instead a manipulative act. Wait until you feel better about yourself. Take care of yourself. Ask for the help you need. Notice where you are. Be more open to accepting your own second chances. Your spirit will be restored in time. With that renewed energy, you will know just what to do to pay it forward.

What If My Workplace Is Toxic: Does Paying It Forward Stand a Chance?

Negativity, gossip, whining, back-biting, and other dysfunctions harm morale and defeat direct communication in some organizations. If the boss is the problem, changing the organizational culture is difficult and likely impossible for an employee. Honestly, toxic environments defeat most attempts at paying it forward. Employees are too fearful to trust an act of kindness.

To listen to my conversation with Jack Gabarro, "Leading the Leader: 3 Rules for Managing Your Boss," go to www .bamradionetwork .com and type "Jack Gabarro" into the search box. For more information, you can also read my 2014 *Exchange* article, "If Your Boss Is the Problem, What Choices Do You Have?"

Toxic environments are not conducive to most of the second-chance strategies discussed in this chapter. Constructive people often see their only option is to find another job. If this is not possible, the employee has a few options. She can decide to do her job well while managing (but having as little involvement as possible in) the charged political environment around her. She can also attempt to hammer out a workable relationship with her boss. She would be ill-informed, however, to go over her boss's head for relief. As Jack Gabarro, Harvard Business School professor, warns, "make sure all the stars are aligned" before risking that path (Gabarro and Snider, "Leading the Leader").

In these nearly impossible settings, the wisest way to pay it forward is to take care of yourself. Pay it forward to yourself by treating yourself with soothing kindness and understanding. Remember that sometimes the most difficult situations are thinly veiled invitations to take that second chance for yourself: Move on, branch out, and open yourself to possibilities you never would have. And remember to keep your sense of humor intact when all about you is going mad.

The Power of Humor, Laughter, and Play in Creating a Culture of Second Chances

The team that laughs together stays together. Laughter is the shortest distance between two people unless we are laughing at (and thereby excluding) another person. Laughter quickly unites us with the people around us. If we can laugh at ourselves, we have little to worry about. When we take ourselves too seriously, we lose our birthright to joy. A lighthearted team is a productive team. A downhearted team is not.

Humor, laughter, and joy are all thresholds to second chances. When you think about it, humor is just another way to regain perspective. When I laugh at my own mistakes, I regain the energy to set things right. When I lighten up, I can notice where I am to see the beauty in the everyday things around me. When I accept my own humanity, I unshackle myself from perfectionism.

In each of these ways, I free myself to see and accept a second chance. Those around me are heartened. Without intending to, I have paid it forward. I have joyously helped create a culture of second chances.

Stuart Brown, play expert, notes, "When people are able to find that sense of play in their work, they become truly powerful figures" (2009, 154).

Enjoying All of It

One more way of creating a culture of second chances is literally to enjoy the richness of ethnicity and cultures around us. What a gift we have as educators: children and their families are each different, each new to us, and each offering new ways to see the world.

As a teacher, I know that even the addition of one new child to the classroom changes the entire classroom: that child brings a whole new world. As a manager, I know that my teams are only as strong as they are diverse. President Lincoln modeled how to do this: He named people to his cabinet who opposed him. In that way, Lincoln could access in a heartbeat any opposition his policies would face. In that way, Lincoln could also learn from his opposition. In that way, by being open to the second chance that comes with listening, Lincoln and his colleagues did far more cocreating than blocking. Our world forever changed as a result.

Reflection Questions

1. Embracing the differences between people is a great ideal. In reality, we are not all Lincolns, able to face every day surrounded by people who take issue with us. As an educator, what lessons have you learned from your experience with children, families, and colleagues about cocreating a learning community that welcomes differences? Have you given

yourself a second chance when you have failed to be as open as you would want?

2. Ms. L'amora has the energy and intention to make a difference in an anonymous way. What power does she have to accomplish her goal of paying it forward? Do you believe she can make a difference? What can she do if some staff resent or are threatened by her? Are you or have you been in L'amora's position?

3. Humor doesn't come as easily to some of us as it does to others. My colleague Luis Hernandez advises us to learn how to lighten up by taking a look at ourselves: we'll find so many quirks and eccentricities that we will have a truckload of reasons to laugh. Who models for you the ability to take herself with a grain of salt? When have you been successful at that? How does a lighthearted workplace (or family) create a treasure trove of second chances?

4. What are the practical, ethical, financial, and even possible legal issues involved in paying it forward? How would you address each one of these issues without losing your enthusiasm for giving back to your team?

5. Can paying it forward set your team up for expecting more and more surprises? I know a director whose staff ended up expecting gifts and parties. The director said she no longer enjoyed paying it forward in this way. The surprise had gone out of the process; entitlement replaced wonder. Staff complained they weren't getting enough. The director's own generosity had gotten in her way. What would you recommend this director do with her staff to bring back the wonder?

6. If called in as a consultant to help a toxic organization, where would you start? What steps would you take? Do you believe toxic organizations can be turned around? If you have worked in a dysfunctional environment, what did you learn from that experience that might help give others a second chance?

Chapter 12

Capitalizing on Our Brain's Evolution toward Second Chances

Your capacity to love others depends entirely on your capacity to love yourself, and take care of yourself.—*Thich Nhat Hanh*

So what do you say? With the tools and tips from the previous chapters available to you, what will be your next move? Will you welcome the next second chance that knocks on your door? Will you actively seek out other second chances? Or will you feel obliged to keep your head down, getting through daily life as you know it? Think about it. In the meantime, consider the following research about the human brain and on our evolution as human beings.

There is no such thing in anyone's life as an unimportant day.
—Alexander Woollcott

Our Brain's Evolution toward Second Chances

Hang in there as you read neuroscientist Sara Morrison and colleagues' research findings below. Yes, the article was written for an audience of neuroscientists, but I promise it's worthwhile to wade through it. What they have to say has a direct correlation to our ability to give and accept second chances. Take a deep breath, reference the key to terminology below as needed, and read on. Okay, I'll meet you on the other side.

Key:

- OFC = orbitofrontal cortex
- PFC = prefrontal cortex
- LFP = local field potential

One distinctive role for OFC may come into play only after learning about reinforcement contingencies. After learning, we found that OFC neurons consistently signal impending reinforcement more rapidly than amygdala. This may reflect the primary role of PFC in executive functions and emotional regulation with regard to both rewarding and aversive experiences. Consistent with this idea, Granger causality analysis of LFP signals *suggests a greater influence of OFC processing on amygdala than the opposite, an effect that emerges with learning.* This effect was especially prominent in the beta frequency band, which has been suggested to be well-suited for long-range interactions between brain areas (Kopell et al. 2000, as cited in Morrison et al. 2011). Importantly, despite the directional effect, the analysis of LFP *data suggests continuous and dynamic reciprocal interactions between OFC and amygdala during task engagement.* We note that this finding does not exclude the possibility that a third brain area—such as another area of PFC—could influence both OFC and amygdala in a consistently asymmetric manner. (Morrison et al. 2011; emphasis added)

What on Earth?

So what does this have to do with anything we educators deal with on a daily basis? For Pete's sake, just say it! What's the point?

When I read neuroscientific studies like this, I flash back to being a young law student, poring over obtuse cases, struggling to mine meaning out of legalese. My brain spikes into a similar rarefied state as I concentrate to plumb out the main point of this recent study on the relationship between the amygdala and the orbitofrontal cortex. I want to know what Morrison and her colleagues have learned about how our brain works. Has their research kicked old beliefs to the curb? Does our executive function have more power over the amygdala than the amygdala has over the executive function? Are we evolving toward hope and spirituality?

I remind myself that each body of knowledge from neuroscience to law to early childhood education has its own language and its own assumptions.

Give Yourself a Break

Your story matters. I mean that. Your story matters to me. Your voice deserves to be heard. If you feel you might want to share your story of second chances with me, I will listen fully. You can text, call, email, or comment on the Redleaf blog. I'm here. I'll get back to you. I will learn from you. I thank you. I wish you joy. Reach me via www.hollyelissabruno .com.

If I can translate the unfamiliar into something to which I can relate, I can make sense of the research. Phrases like "consistent asymmetry" take me down alleyways of my imagination: my brain is always attracted to/distracted by novel, somewhat off-center possibilities. Does "consistent asymmetry" suggest unevenness and that imbalance is more common than perfection and predictability? Hmmmm.

Fortunately, I have a translator in Mickey Goldberg, otherwise known as Michael E. Goldberg, who is a colleague of the study's authors at Columbia University. At heart Goldberg is a teacher, skilled at explaining how monkey brain studies can deepen human understanding. I asked Goldberg what the latest important findings are on the executive function's ability to "partner with" the amygdala. In everyday terms, I wanted Goldberg's help with the question, Can the reflective and reactive parts of our brains cooperate so that challenges can be processed more readily as opportunities? In other words, can fear clear the way toward hope?

And what I understood Goldberg to say in response was "Yes."

Yes? Hooray! Our brains are evolving toward integration of fear and hope. Instead of our amygdala slamming us into that defensive "back off!" crouched position, with the help of our prefrontal cortex, the amygdala can telegraph messages of "Pay attention! Herein lies a second chance!" How sweet is that?

The Brain's Evolution to Be in the World but Not Destroyed by It

Here's the skinny: Our executive function is quicker to transform threat messages from the amygdala into "Pay attention to the moment. Here's a possibility you need to consider. Now!" It is quicker to call our attention to "Okay, you may be scared. But hold on. Here's something new for you: Breathe through the fear, and something better may be waiting for you on the other side."

Now I understand why another neuroscientist, Louis Cozolino, author of *The Neuroscience of Human Relationships* (2014), told me that as we mature, the executive function and the amygdala build pathways so that our buttons don't get pushed as much. Cozolino posits that we are set up neurologically to grow wise as we age (Cozolino, "3 Keys to Leading People Who Push Your Buttons").

In essence, our brains are rewiring our responses to troubles by encouraging us to pay attention to possibility and to rely upon our hard-earned skills of stepping back, defusing our fear, and using the stimulation of more adrenaline to focus on what is meaningful. At the same time, our brain is:

- getting over the need for either/or thinking (either I run for the hills, or I smack my enemy upside the head);
- positioning us instead to notice where we are; and
- offering us more capability to discover the second chance awaiting us.

Choosing Joy over Fear, Courage over Denial

At heart, our brains are rewiring themselves to find second chances. Neuroscientists might not put it that way, but I will. Cozolino supports my optimism when, during our conversation, he observes: "As we get older, the amygdala seems to be more gentle with us. We tend to remember more positive things." And as a human race, we are destined toward wisdom, and that's what aging can be about if we choose courage in little ways each day.

Remember the story of Viktor Frankl in chapter 8? Frankl witnessed and experienced unthinkable tragedies while imprisoned in a World War II concentration camp. He lost his beloved wife and his young son. Why was he still alive? Why were others still alive?

He looked around him. Who was surviving these wrenching atrocities? Who found resilience? Who could notice even the most fleeting rays of hope? The survivors, he noticed, were the people who could help others, offer them the comfort of little things, offer just enough optimism to soothe their exhausted spirits. Frankl became one of those people. He survived to tell the story.

Choose our attitude. In any given set of circumstances, choose to lift our heads. Choose to step back and step out of harm's way. Choose to help another person. Choose to lighten up on ourselves. Choose to look more deeply. Choose hope over despair. Choose to return to our fountain of second chances. Choose a spiritual pathway. Dive deeper for the pearls.

Comfort in Little Things

Think of a song that lifts your heart with joy and soothing, a song you might share with someone who is hurting. If you don't know the song by heart, find the music online.

Claim time by yourself today in a place where no one can break into your privacy.

Now sing that song. Who cares about your "solo voice?" Sing that song for you. Play that song for you. May that anthem release a sigh or smile or tear of knowing that you are always worthy.

You alone can sing the lullaby your heart needs most.

Our Brain on a Spiritual Quest

Remember, for the purposes of this book, spirituality is seeking a life of deeper meaning. For some, their religious pathway is their spiritual pathway. For others, practicing the Twelve Steps to recovery is their spirituality. For others, no external pathway suffices. Some do rely on a higher power, Great Spirit, God, angels, or saints. I'm good with all of this. Like respecting cultural differences and honoring every person's individualities, I prefer to honor religious (and nonreligious) differences.

Even without differences in our spiritual beliefs, what each of us has in common is our deep desire to live a meaningful life and to leave the world in a better way than we found it. Our deep desire is to claim and offer second chances so that we can all enjoy and co-create a far-reaching and embracing learning community. What each of us has in common is our desire to make a difference, despite (and/or because of) adversity from the outside and limitation from the inside.

Those who reflect on their life in a spiritual sense believe they are on a pathway toward some form of salvation. Salvation is the process of triumphing over evil and seeking to be and do what's kind and good. We give salvation different names such as heaven, release from purgatory, a good life, nirvana, heaven on earth, grace, bodhisattva status, and human kindness.

Salvation by any definition requires the student (seeker or pilgrim) to face the most gripping of fears and triumph over those fears with the hope that comes from faith in the sacred. How brilliant that our brains are now aligned with our quest toward meaning. How brilliant that, as Frost stated in his poem "Mending Wall," "something there is that doesn't love a wall." Something there is inside of us that prefers learning to labeling and understanding to warfare. Something there is within us that cries out to claim second chances as our birthright.

If this is the case, let's pull together the spiritual principles throughout this book that lead us to second chances. Consider these guidelines and practices. Note that many of these come from poets, prophets, soothsayers (truth tellers), theologians, and everyday early childhood heroes:

* When we are in the presence of a spiritual person, hope rises up in us.
* Courage to face our fears is the source of serenity.
* We are souls enfleshed, on a spiritual pathway.

- The hounds of heaven will pursue us unless we step up to becoming who we are meant to be.
- Our hearts and intuitions work together with our inner voices as our guides.
- Discernment is a lifelong challenge and opportunity.
- Be present in the moment to see the present in the moment.
- It's never too late to have a happy childhood.
- Life's too short to do anything but enjoy it daily.
- Don't let the turkeys (self-doubt, naysayers, critical people, worriers) get you down. Discouragement is acid on our souls.
- Paying it forward is what we are on Earth to do.
- Live so that when you come to the end of your life, you will not discover that you have not lived.
- Waiting for you now are second chances. Look up to notice where you are.
- Fill in the blank with other spiritual principles that guide you:

_____

Practical Spiritual Principles on the Pathway to Second Chances

Listen to adjunct instructor Margaret Jones's description of her choices with her students. When Margaret was criticized by a student, she could have allowed herself to fall prey to negative criticism, self-doubt, or self-pity. She took that criticism personally at first. Watch how she evolves from woundedness to strength, from hopelessness to happiness, and from disconnection to deeper connection.

I teach courses at the university level in early childhood administration and Leadership. I have some very knowledgeable students in my courses who have many years of experience in the field of early care and education. I wholeheartedly believe I often learn as much from them as they learn from me.

I typically teach at night because that is when my students are not at work. I tend to be a "morning" person and rise early, just as they do, and it frequently has been a long day by the time we are in class together. By that point in the day, our "emotional intelligence" is waning, or at least, I know mine is. I may not always be as aware of how student's comments and questions are affecting me until the next morning when I am reflecting on how the class went the night before.

One night I had a student who has taken several courses with me, and whom I know to be very astute, ask me why an assignment was set up the way it was. She expressed that it was not written clearly and that she did not receive the score she had worked so hard to get on that assignment because it was vague and not worded effectively. My first reaction was not defensive but, instead, apologetic. I trusted that she had thoroughly read the rubric for the assignment and because I had not written it effectively, she was penalized. I trusted her judgment was not meant to hurt me, but it made me question myself and my ability as an instructor.

I believe it was my emotional state of being tired after a long day that lowered my confidence in myself. I took her comments and criticism personally. I asked some of the other students in the class if they had the same experience with the assignment in question. They agreed that the wording was not easy for them to understand. With that, I was sure I would have an apology to make and an assignment to rewrite and scores to recalculate.

Fortunately, I had the presence of mind to pull up the assignment document. Our classes meet via web-conferencing, and I can share any document from my computer with the class at any time. We read the assignment carefully together. There was one word that was actually there in the description that this student and others had missed when they read the assignment. That one word made all the difference in how they interpreted what was expected for the assignment. It was the one thing that was missing in this student's assignment, which brought down her score.

As it turned out, she was the one to apologize and asked if she could resubmit her assignment. I was happy to offer that opportunity. I learned that when

I am tired, I tend to take things more personally than I should. At those times I need to remember a response I learned from my son years ago: "Give me some time to think about that."

—Margaret Jones, July 17, 2014

As you read Margaret's story, what did you hear that might help you? Did her experience sound familiar to you in any way?

Margaret's observation reminded me to do the following:

- Let go of perfectionism.
- Relax my ego; listen to the feedback.
- Sleep on it.
- Apologize for my wrongdoing.
- Make amends.
- Remind myself that I am okay throughout all of this; I learn from mistakes.
- Continue learning.

And now Sue's story. Sue is a Head Start teacher who never gives up on students. For Shanda, a student is always brilliant in his own way, even if the student is doing his best to cover up his brilliance. Read Sue's story below and my response as she and I work together to understand what second chances are all about.

Dear Holly,

The second chance that I would like to share is about a past student of mine. I first met J. when he was in my Head Start class. I was the center manager and lead teacher; he was four and I was obviously attached to him as I was with many children. Through the years I have watched J. grow into a young man. I have loved him and encouraged him, despite his poor choices and trouble with the law. Because we live in a very small town, I am able to see him often. When I do, I hug him, tell him I believe in him, and encourage him.

A few years ago his father died from a drug and alcohol overdose. He came to me and wanted to talk. However, since that time he continues to be in trouble, as well as his two other siblings. I gave him a promise that I would never give up on him. I have told him that despite his poor choices, I will love him, support him, and give him honest advice to help him succeed in life. Recently he went back to an alternative high school.

I hope that J. knows that there are very few people who he has pulling for him but that my support may be his second chance. I just hope that he will grasp the hand that is reaching out to him. I hope that I can share down the road what a successful young man he has become. But for now, I will love him right where he is.

—Sue Marks, March 27, 2014

My response:

You are a marvel, Ms. Sue. Your love for J. will always be in his heart. Trust me.

My elementary teacher, Michael Gonta, saved my life. He was the first and only person who believed in me. He saw me. To this day, I love him back . . . to the moon and back!

Like J., I didn't make great decisions. Took me a long time to believe I was worthy and not destined to repeat "the sins of the fathers."

Forty years later, I was able to find Mr. Gonta and thank him. In fact, I dedicated my book *What You Need to Lead* to him. When I need advice, I turn to him.

J. has one person in his corner, for always. Never doubt the gift you have given him.

When we give a child a second chance, we give that child hope for a lifetime.

Thank you for making a difference, one J. at a time.

—Holly Elissa, March 28, 2014

What does hearing Sue's story inspire in you? For sure, she inspired me to recall a pivotal experience in my life. And to have gratitude for one very special teacher, who at eighty-six remains one of my closest friends. Never doubt the grace of being an educator: we are in the business of second chances.

What Choice Will You (and I) Make?

Yes. In this year of second chances I have said yes to every second chance I was aware of, and some I wasn't aware of. Shakespeare advises, "The readiness is all." Even if we don't consciously notice the second chance in front of us, our readiness to grow allows us to do just that even if we aren't aware of our curiosity or where it might take us. I intend to live my life deeply and fully and happily. I believe that intention invites possibilities.

Along the way in this year of readiness, I have offered as many second chances to others as I could. Sometimes I just stilled myself in a person's presence to listen with my heart and any other faculty I could call on. Sometimes, I asked to hear more. Other times I gave words to my understanding of what was aching to be said.

Those moments were unanticipated clearings in otherwise busy days, moments where what matters became clearer, where truth could be told and understanding deepened. Perhaps decisions for freedom were made. Or maybe we both experienced that precious timelessness of being fully heard. True selves, fully heard, fully accepted. Our perfectly imperfect selves were more than up for the challenge.

I also accepted these moments for myself whenever I had the awareness. Whenever I felt something was roiling around inside me that needed to be heard. Whenever I was at odds within myself. Or taken by something I had heard or seen. I would stop, notice where I was internally, and write as much of the truth as I could bear to write. Most of the writing I did in these moments would become the blog posts for this book.

One July morning, just after sunrise, I looked out over my gardens to the lake and wrote the following.

Hounds of Heaven

This second chance that is making the rounds inside me is not a daily second chance.

I love those daily second chances that emerge because I stop to notice where I am: entranced by the movement of a woolly caterpillar, transfixed by the cherry pink peony's ebullience, fascinated by my young son's question, "What happens to God when I die?"

I love second chances that bloom out of paying it forward: Witnessing the surprised delight of an older couple when they discover someone unknown has paid for their rare "date night" dinner out. Witnessing wonder in the eyes of a child of refugees when she wins a full scholarship to college. Witnessing a teacher gasp upon finding a vase of red roses in her classroom. Watching the slow smile of the next customer at the coffee shop when he hears, "Your order has been taken care of, sir."

Every second chance I have witnessed or experienced is a momentary miracle. A moment of awe and gratitude. Timelessness and humility. A moment to see with the eyes of a child.

But this second chance that is making the rounds inside me is not a daily second chance. This yet-to-be-formed second chance is a life changer. A knock-your-socks-off, not-know-what-hit-you, shout "Hallelujah!" second chance. I know this. I feel this. I have felt this before at defining points in my life.

I felt this when, to confront my fear of heights, I leapt off the platform of a zip line tautly stretched above the Guatemalan jungle. I felt this when I accepted McGraw-Hill's offer to write a textbook I didn't believe I could write. I felt this when I received a photograph of a ten-month-old, wild-haired "No-I-won't-hold-still-for-this-picture" boy from Anyang, Korea; if I said yes to the adoption agency, that baby would become my forever son.

Then as now, I have little sense of what lies ahead. I am not a bungee-jumping, rock-climbing Acapulco diver. These days I prefer serenity to drama, having experienced ample drama to last a few lifetimes. I am sixty-eight and a half years old, for Pete's sake. Wouldn't I be smarter to live out my life surrounded with hard-earned comforts and familiar pathways?

Smarter? Probably.

Wiser? No.

I said yes then and I will say yes now. To say no would be to cut off an arm or deny a dream.

I'm scared. I'm worried (and I am not the worrying type). I don't look forward to the rupture big changes seem to require. This time I will prepare better. I'll level with my friends, as I am leveling with you. I'll ask for help. I'll pray. I'll even consider doing "damage control" for the first time.

And when I'm ready, I will leap. Today I know this. Tomorrow, or even later today, I might chicken out. But eventually I will leap.

The hounds of heaven will nip at my ankles and yelp to the stars until I say yes. I know how this goes. I know the risks. I know the joy. I will accept my second chance for a truer, simpler, and more sacred life.

—Holly Elissa, July 30, 2014

Have the hounds of heaven nipped and yelped at you? If so, how on earth did or will you make your choice? What awaited or awaits you on the other side?

My Year of Second Chances

Want to know what happened as a result of my devoting a year to second chances?

Here are moments I've had in this year of deep transition with all its attendant wonder and fear:

- Watermelon pink, deep-night purple, all POP! into my night. I am in India, where color is beyond color.

- I say good-bye to my country home of fifteen years and hello to sunlight splashing through the oversized windows of my urban, 1890s apartment.

- Having always lived with other people (from sisters to roommates to husbands and partners), for the first time in my life, I live solo in my own apartment, pleasing no one but myself.

- Today is my day; every experience in my life has brought me here. I know a new freedom and I am finding my way home.

Choosing to Live Deeply and Happily

Today, in this moment, and in the most unexpected of moments, you will be presented with a second chance to live more deeply with more authenticity and more joy. This does not mean you will always have an easy path. It does not mean you will have easy choices. The hounds of heaven will nip at you, and like me, sometimes you will chicken out. It's all okay.

What matters is that you know that what awaits you when you are ready is beauty you never imagined and insights that will light the rest of your way.

Life's too short and too precious to do anything but enjoy it daily. May your days abound with second chances and your heart be strong and vulnerable enough to choose the unseen and the unknown. Therein lies majesty.

Resources

Allan, Trish. "9 Self-Care Essentials to Add to Your Life." *Mind Body Green.*
November 10, 2013. http://www.mindbodygreen.com/0-11589/9-self-care-essentials-to
-add-to-your-life.html.

Bergman, Peter. "If You're Too Busy to Meditate, Read This." *Harvard
Business Review*, October 12, 2012. http://blogs.hbr.org/2012/10/
if-youre-too-busy-to-meditate/

Blair, Ann. "Information Overload Is Not Unique to Digital Age." Interview by Tony
Cox. National Public Radio. November 29, 2010.

Bruno, Holly Elissa. "Hold the Phone! Cell Phone Policies Prevent Harm to
Children." *Exchange*, (September/October, 2014): 14–18.

———. "If Your Boss Is the Problem, What Choices Do You Have?" *Exchange*,
November/December, 2014: 16–24.

Center for Spiritual Intelligence. http://spiritualintelligence.com.

Dillard-Wright, David. "How to Find Time to Meditate." *Mindful: Taking Time for
What Matters*. Excerpt from *Meditation for Multitaskers: Your Guide to Finding
Peace between the Pings* by David Dillard-Wright. http://www.mindful.org
/mindfulness-practice/meditation-in-action/scheduled-meditation.

Ditty, Ann, Suzanne Eckes, Sue Offutt, and Lee Kolbert. "Creating Sensible Policies
on Cell Phones in the Classroom." Interview by Holly Elissa Bruno. *Heart to Heart
Conversations on Leadership: Your Guide to Making a Difference*. BAM! Radio.
Podcast audio. http://www.bamradionetwork.com/index.php?option=com
_content&view=article&id=1068:jackstreet54&catid=36:administrators
-channel&Itemid=90.

Dixit, Jay. "The Art of Now: Six Steps to Living in the Moment." *Psychology Today*,
November 10, 2008. http://www.psychologytoday.com/articles/200810
/the-art-now-six-steps-living-in-the-moment.

"Eleanor Roosevelt Biography." *Bio.* http://www.biography.com/people
/eleanor-roosevelt-9463366.

Engel, Beverly. "How to Give a Meaningful Apology." UMass Amherst Family
Business Center. 2002. http://www.umass.edu/fambiz/articles/resolving_conflict
/meaningful_apology.html.

Fox, MeiMei. "40 Ways to Find Joy in Your Everyday Life." *The Blog: Huffington Post*, January 10, 2013 (updated March 11, 2013). http://www.huffingtonpost.com /meimei-fox/happiness-tips_b_2405608.html.

Frankl, Viktor. "Why Believe in Other." Speech given at Toronto Youth Corps, May 1972. *TED Talks*. http://www.ted.com/talks/viktor_frankl_youth_in_search _of_meaning.

Friedman, Stew, Marquita Davis, Nancy Blair, and Dwight Carter. "Driven, Consumed, and Overwhelmed: Stepping toward Balance." Interview by Holly Elissa Bruno. *Heart to Heart Conversations on Leadership: Your Guide to Making a Difference*. BAM! Radio. Podcast audio. http://www.bamradionetwork.com /index.php?option=com_content&view=article&id=2231:driven-consumed -and-overwhelmed-stepping-toward-balance-&catid=36:administrators -channel&Itemid=90.

"Frozen Body: Can We Return from the Dead?" *BBC: Science,* August 15, 2013. http://www.bbc.co.uk/science/0/23695785.

Goleman, Daniel. *Primal Leadership: Unleashing the Power of Emotional Intelligence*. Boston: Harvard Business Review Press, 2013.

Hendrikson, Ellen. "How to Stop Avoiding Conflict." *QuickandDirtyTips*.com, April 4, 2014. http://www.quickanddirtytips.com/health-fitness/mental-health /how-to-stop-avoiding-conflict.

Higgins, Chris. "20 Gentle Quotation from Mister Rogers." *Mental Floss*. December 17, 2012. http://mentalfloss.com/article/31936/20-gentle-quotations -mister-rogers.

Larsen, Britta, and Susan Offutt. "Get Over It! Managing Grudges in Education Settings." Interview by Holly Elissa Bruno. *Heart to Heart Conversations on Leadership: Your Guide to Making a Difference*. BAM! Radio. Podcast audio. http://www.bamradionetwork.com/index.php?option=com_content&view =article&id=884:leadr&catid=69:infobamradionetworkcom&Itemid=144.

"Making Amends Is More Than an Apology." *Hazelden Betty Ford Foundation*. http://www.hazelden.org/web/public/has70305.page.

Marshall, Tess. "How to Give Yourself a Second Chance." *The Bold Life: Inspiration for Fearless Living* (blog). October 2011. http://theboldlife.com/2011/10 /give-chance/.

"Placido Domingo and Andrea Bocelli – Pearl Fishers duet," *YouTube*, 6:33, from the performance at Arena di Verona on June 1, 2013, posted by "mareliel," June 11, 2013, https://www.youtube.com/watch?v=i-v-DZjZ9iY.

Plante, Thomas. "Can You Teach Compassion?" *Do the Right Thing* (blog). *Psychology Today.* January 22, 2014. http://www.psychologytoday.com/blog/do-the-right -thing/201401/can-you-teach-compassion.

"Profiles of the Sixteen Personality Types." *Truity.* http://www.truity.com/view /types.

"PTSD in Children and Teens." *PTSD: National Center for PTSD*. U.S. Department of Veteran Affairs. January 3, 2014. http://www.ptsd.va.gov/public/family/ptsd-children-adolescents.asp.

Seiberg, Daniel. *The Digital Diet: The 4-Step Plan to Break Your Tech Addiction and Regain Balance in Your Life*. New York: Three Rivers Press, 2011.

Share Your Stories! (blog). Redleaf Press. http://redleafpressblog.org.

"Sigmund Freud (1856–1939)." *Internet Encyclopedia of Philosophy*. http://www.iep.utm.edu/freud/.

Substance Abuse and Mental Health Services Administration, U.S. Department of Health and Human Services: Strengthening Families Program. June 2007. https://store.samhsa.gov/shin/content/SVP07-0186/SVP07-0186.pdf.

Williams, Ray B. "Why We Don't Keep Our New Year's Resolutions." *Wired for Success* (blog). *Psychology Today*. December 21, 2013. http://www.psychologytoday.com/blog/wired-success/201312/why-we-dont-keep-our-new-years-resolutions.

References

"Adverse Childhood Experiences Reported by Adults—Five States, 2009." Centers for Disease Control and Prevention. *Morbidity and Mortality Weekly Report (MMWR)* 59, no. 49 (December 17, 2010): 1609–13. http://www.cdc.gov/mmwr/preview/mmwrhtml/mm5949a1.htm

Beauvoir, Simone de. 2011. *The Second Sex.* New York: Vintage Books.

Bellow, Saul. 1996. *The Victim.* New York: Penguin Classics.

Blake, William. 1901; Project Gutenberg 2008. *Songs of Innocence and Songs of Experience.* London: R. Brimley Johnson. http://www.gutenberg.org/files/1934/1934-h/1934-h.htm

Brown, Stuart. 2009. *Play: How It Shapes the Brain, Opens the Imagination, and Invigorates the Soul.* New York: Penguin.

Browning, Robert. 1899; Project Gutenberg 2005. *Browning's Shorter Poems,* ed Franklin T. Baker. New York: Macmillan. http://www.gutenberg.org/files/16376/16376-h/16376-h.htm

Bruno, Holly Elissa. 2012. *What You Need to Lead an Early Childhood Program: Emotional Intelligence in Practice.* Washington, DC: National Association for the Education of Young Children.

Bruno, Holly Elissa, and Tom Copeland. 2012. *Managing Legal Risks in Early Childhood Programs: How to Prevent Flare-Ups from Becoming Lawsuits.* New York: Teachers College Press.

Bryant, Adam. 2011. *The Corner Office: Indispensable and Unexpected Lessons from CEOs on How to Lead and Succeed.* New York: Times Books.

Burns, Ken. 2014. *The Roosevelts: An Intimate History.* Walpole, NH: Florentine Films. Broadcast by PBS. http://www.pbs.org/kenburns/films/the-roosevelts.

Chance, Zoë, Lisa Dabbs, and Jessica Johnson. "Too Little Time?: Find More Time in Unexpected Places." Interview by Holly Elissa Bruno. *Heart to Heart Conversations on Leadership: Your Guide to Making a Difference.* BAM! Radio. Podcast audio. http://www.bamradionetwork.com/directors-and-administrators-channel/916-too-little-time-find-more-time-in-unexpected-places.

Chesler, Phyllis. 2009. *Woman's Inhumanity to Woman.* Chicago: Lawrence Hill Books.

Cozolino, Louis. 2014. *The Neuroscience of Human Relationships: Attachment and the Developing Social Brain.* 2nd ed. New York: W. W. Norton.

———. "3 Keys to Leading People Who Push Your Buttons." Interview by Holly Elissa Bruno. *Heart to Heart Conversations on Leadership: Your Guide to Making a Difference.* BAM! Radio. Podcast audio. http://www.bamradionetwork.com /index.php?option=com_content&view=article&id=413:jackstreet54&catid=69 :infobamradionetworkcom&Itemid=144.

Engel, Beverly. 2002. "The Power of Apology." *Psychology Today*, July 1. http://www .psychologytoday.com/articles/200208/the-power-apology.

Forrester, Michelle M., and Kay M. Albrecht. 2014. *Social Emotional Tools for Life: An Early Childhood Teacher's Guide to Supporting Strong Emotional Foundations and Successful Social Relationships.* Tomball, TX: Innovations in ECE Press.

Frankl, Viktor. 1959. *Man's Search for Meaning.* Cutchogue, NY: Buccaneer Books.

Frost, Robert. 1915; Project Gutenberg 2009. *North of Boston.* New York: Henry Holt and Company. http://www.gutenberg.org/files/3026/3026-h/3026-h.htm

Gabarro, Jack, and Justin Snider. "Leading the Leader: 3 Rules for Managing Your Boss" Interview by Holly Elissa Bruno. *Heart to Heart Conversations on Leadership: Your Guide to Making a Difference.* BAM! Radio. Podcast audio. http://www.bamradionetwork.com/directors-and-administrators-channel /587-leading-the-leader-3-rules-for-managing-your-boss.

Gardner, Howard. 1999. *Intelligence Reframed: Multiple Intelligences for the 21st Century.* New York: Basic Books.

———. 2011. *Frames of Mind: The Theory of Multiple Intelligences.* 3rd ed. New York: Basic Books.

Goleman, Daniel. 1995. *Emotional Intelligence: Why It Can Matter More Than IQ.* New York: Bantam Dell.

Goleman, Daniel, Richard Boyatzis, and Annie McKee. 2013. *Primal Leadership: Unleashing the Power of Emotional Intelligence.* Boston: Harvard Business Review Press.

Hanh, Thich Nhat. 2001. *Anger: Wisdom for Cooling the Flames.* New York: Riverhead Books.

James, William. (1902) 2012. Edited by Matthew Bradley. Oxford: Oxford World's Classics. *The Varieties of Religious Experience: A Study in Human Nature.*

Keats, John. 1820; Project Gutenberg 2007. *Lamia, Isabella, The Eve of St. Agnes, and Other Poems.* London: Taylor and Hessey. http://www.gutenberg.org/ files/23684/23684-h/23684-h.htm.

Kellerman, Barbara. 2006. "When Should a Leader Apologize and When Not?" *Harvard Business Review* 84, no. 4 (April): 72–81. https://hbr.org/2006/04 /when-should-a-leader-apologize-and-when-not/ar/1.

Kellerman, Barbara, and Justin Snider. "When and How to Say, 'I Was Wrong.'" Interview by Holly Elissa Bruno. *Heart to Heart Conversations on Leadership:*

Your Guide to Making a Difference. BAM! Radio. Podcast audio. http://www
.bamradionetwork.com/index.php?option=com_content&view=article&id=430
:jackstreet54&catid=69:infobamradionetworkcom&Itemid=144.

Lee, Gus, and George Couras, with Holly Elissa Bruno. "Do You Have the Courage
to Be an Effective Educational Leader?" BAM! Radio. Podcast audio. http://www
.bamradionetwork.com/index.php?option=com_content&view=article&id=537
:jackstreet54&catid=36:administrators-channel&Itemid=90.

Levitin, Daniel J. 2014. "Hit the Reset Button in Your Brain." *New York Times*, Sunday
Review Opinion, August 9. http://www.nytimes.com/2014/08/10/opinion
/sunday/hit-the-reset-button-in-your-brain.html?_r=0.

Maslow, Abraham. 1970. *Motivation and Personality*. 2nd ed. New York: Harper and
Row.

McLeod, Saul. 2007. "Maslow's Hierarchy of Needs." *Simply Psychology* (updated
2014). http://www.simplypsychology.org/maslow.html.

Medina, John J., Jim Sporleder, Peter DeWitt, and Deborah J. Stewart. "Creating
Safe Learning Spaces for Traumatized Children." Interview by Holly Elissa Bruno.
Heart to Heart Conversations on Leadership: Your Guide to Making a Difference.
BAM! Radio. Podcast audio. http://www.bamradionetwork.com/index
.php?option=com_content&view=article&id=1190:jackstreet54&catid=36
:administrators-channel&Itemid=90.

Melville, Herman. 1851. *Moby-Dick*. Bantam Classic edition 1981. New York: Bantam
Dell.

Morrison, Sara E., Alexander Saez, Brian Lau, and C. Daniel Salzman. 2011.
"Different Time Courses for Learning-Related Changes in Amygdala and
Orbitofrontal Cortex." *Neuron* 71, no. 6 (September 22): 1127–40. doi:10.1016
/j.neuron.2011.07.016.

Myers, Isabel Briggs, Mary H. McCaulley, Naomi L. Quenk, and Allen L. Hammer.
1998. *MBTI Manual: A Guide to the Development and Use of the Myers-Briggs Type
Indicator*. 3rd ed. Palo Alto: Consulting Psychologists Press.

Nouwen, Henri J.M. 1979. *The Wounded Healer: Ministry in Contemporary Society.*
New York: Image.

Pay it Forward. 2000. Directed by Mimi Leder. Burbank, CA: Warner Brothers
Pictures. DVD.

Rilke, Rainer Maria. 2005. *Rilke's Book of Hours: Love Letters to God*. Translated by
Anita Barrows and Joanna Macy. New York: Berkley Publishing Group.

Rogers, Fred. 2005. *Life's Journeys according to Mister Rogers: Things to Remember
along the Way*. New York: Hachette Books.

Roosevelt, Eleanor. 1960. *You Learn by Living: Eleven Keys for a More Fulfilling Life*.
New York: Harper and Row.

———. 1963. *Tomorrow Is Now*. New York: Harper and Row.

Rosen, Larry D. 2012. *iDisorder: Understanding Our Obsession with Technology and Overcoming Its Hold on Us*. New York: Palgrave Macmillan.

Rosen, Larry, and Steven W. Anderson. "Addicted to Technology: Do We Need a 12 Step Program?" Interview by Holly Elissa Bruno. *Heart to Heart Conversations on Leadership: Your Guide to Making a Difference*. BAM! Radio. Podcast audio. http://www.bamradionetwork.com/index.php?option=com_content&view=article&id=2263:addicted-to-technology-do-we-need-a-12-step-program&catid=36:administrators-channel&Itemid=90.

Starr, Alexandra. 2005. "Subadolescent Queen Bees." *New York Times*, December 11. http://www.nytimes.com/2005/12/11/magazine/11ideas_section4-2.html?_r=0.

Walfisch, Tamar, Dina Van Dijk, and Ronit Kark. 2013. "Do You Really Expect Me to Apologize? The Impact of Status and Gender on the Effectiveness of an Apology in the Workplace." *Journal of Applied Social Psychology* 43, no. 7 (July): 1446–58. doi: 10.1111/jasp.12101.

Woods, Wendy. 2012. "Meditating at Work: A New Approach to Managing Overload." *Noetic Now* 19 (February). http://www.noetic.org/noetic/issue-nineteen-february/meditating-at-work/.